*O Beloved
Being, Becoming,
and Beyond*

-Shunya

Published by Best Seller Publishing®, Pasadena, CA Best Seller Publishing® is a registered trademark Printed in the United States of America.
ISBN 978-1-7352029-3-8

This publication is designed to provide accurate and authoritative information with regard to the subject matter covered. It is sold with the understanding that the publisher is not engaged in rendering legal, accounting, or other professional advice. If legal advice or other expert assistance is required, the services of a competent professional should be sought. The opinions expressed by the authors in this book are not endorsed by Best Seller Publishing® and are the sole responsibility of the author rendering the opinion.

For more information, please write:
Best Seller Publishing®
253 N. San Gabriel Blvd, Unit B
Pasadena, CA 91107
or call 1(626) 765 9750
Visit us online at: www.BestSellerPublishing.org

Dedication Note

This work is dedicated to all those people
who live with a question in their heart to know their essence,
and, to all those who let this question grow into a burning
curiosity, and, to all those who choose to quench this curiosity
with real actions, and to all those who are able
to transform their actions into conscious living.

A conscious *being* is a jewel of existence, through which
the existential truth shines. This work is dedicated to
all conscious *beings*, who were ever born, or living now,
or yet to be born, out of mother earth.
And, this work is dedicated to the vast existential consciousness,
mirrored in all conscious *beings*.

Foreword

This book is a travelogue. It transports us away from our usual pre- occupations and takes us on a series of mini-vacations to places of great beauty and splendor, where our hearts and minds are refreshed and renewed. It is filled with exquisite art that delights the eyes and soothes our whole *being*, inviting us to be present, attentive, and observant. The words carry us like a gentle river to places of new understanding and recognition of things we may have once known—or at least suspected yet have long since forgotten. Like treasures *being* revealed, accompanied by the unique joy of each new revelation.

Shunya accomplishes something rare and remarkable with this book. He takes us on journey after journey, illuminating various aspects of individuality, society, life, and spirit, along with their kaleidoscopic interactions, yet all the while, he manages to keep us grounded and connected to our present reality at the same time. He does this through his preludes to each poem, which create a clear context and a strong foundation, filling us with wonder as we are launched into yet another exquisite adventure of insight.

I felt deeply nourished as I allowed myself to be transported by this book. It was like getting a soul massage. Each reading left my heart lighter and my mind brighter, imbuing my innermost *being* with an incredible, precious, indescribable scent, which I will simply call love.

A book such as this does not need to be described; it needs to be experienced. It is an invitation. It needs to be entered. Honor the invitation, enter without preconceptions, experience the richness that is offered here, and return a little different each time, like a traveler returns, forever transformed by the journey. Enjoy these mini-vacations across the landscape of life, timeless mysteries, and your own innermost *being*.

I am honored to be invited to write this foreword and to call Shunya my friend.

With love and happiness,
Nithya

Acknowledgment

Though the making of this book took a few years, building the mindset to do it has been a lifelong work. And to see that this journey is bringing fruits gives me immense happiness. Honestly, I feel that I am merely a conduit of many contributions, gifted to me.

For this accomplishment, I would like to express my sincere love and deepest gratitude to all those lovely souls who contributed overtly or covertly.

With deep love, respect, and honor, I thank *His Holiness Hardev Singh ji Nirankari,* who was an epitome of purity and compassion. His penetrating teachings have grown the right values in me since my childhood, helping me to attain this inward-looking attitude towards life.

To my beloved parents, *Mr. Chandgi Ram* and *Ms. Vimla Devi,* who are two flames of unconditional love and countless blessings.

To my best friend and wife—*Simpi*—who has been a constant support, and keeps me grounded in the practical aspects of life.

And to all my friends and relatives who instilled constant motivation and trust in me to complete this book.

Finally, with the utmost respect, I want to thank you—*the reader*— who is holding the book, as, without your thought in my mind, I would not have started this work.

Table of Offerings

Introduction
—Being, Becoming, and Beyond

Human life is nothing but a stream of experiences—physical, mental, and spiritual. Even though the nature of the stream is the same for all people, the actual experience of living is unique for everyone.

Without exception, we all seek, create, and consume countless experiences in our unique ways, with one common desire—to live through the best experience. Our entire endeavor is employed to serve this desire. Many of us also name this best experience as "joy" or "happiness."

What is the popular definition of this best experience? And how do we gain it?

Each one of us may have different words, but common answers include wealth, fame, power, and social importance. And, common means are money, society, career, political victory, religions, sports, education, family, and many more arrangements created around us. And, the common graph of achievement is by classification, comparison, competition, identity, and ownership.

In a way, we have organized our happiness into a few labeled boxes, and we compete for their ownership. This hypothesis of happiness and its design is collectively embraced and cunningly enforced at the same time. Of course, its a skill to win the race of maximizing *the predictable joy.*

On rare occasions, accidentally, we have glimpses of experiences deeper than the common stock, which challenge our made-up mind and make us feel deeply connected, in a non-comparative way; like when we are in deep love with someone, or hold a newborn baby to look into her clear innocent eyes, or someone very near to our heart dies and leaves us empty.

But these glimpses fade away very fast because the propaganda of this made-up world and its arrangements is so strong that we have become attached, addicted, and absorbed in it, fully.

It's not a theory, but the practicality of our daily life. When we wake up in the morning, how do we connect to the world? Is it with a fresh sense of existential connectivity or with a worrisome backlog of *to-do* list of social, commercial, political, or religious activities? This backlog continues until we surrender to sleep again in the night, and, many times, it gets rolled down in our dreams. It feels like life has become a task, and the joy of living is nothing, but the achievement of tasks.

It is not by surprise that we like life stories that are full of the dramatic seesaw between stress and success; they make sense to us because we live the similar stressful drama in our daily life. It informs us about the quality of our life experience. Doesn't it?

Unfortunately, many of us spend the entire lifetime, in the teeter- totter of this superficially made-up world. Isn't it a time to press pause and question our daily living? Are we living to solve this teeter-totter or to feel deeply the connection with real existence?

The truth is that deeply connected life experiences are more fulfilling; at the same time they are difficult to express and generally label-less. The key is to look inward and self-study.

An immediate reward of sincere self-study is a clear mind and an undistorted perception, which transforms our perspective postively about reality of life. This positivity comes with inner joy, enhanced receptivity, recycling of borrowed identity into individuality, and oneness with existence.

Now, the most important question arises, how to materialize the intention of self-study into our practical life?

Let's look at our day to day life—dynamic and situational. Sometimes it feels like a silent river in the countryside, or another time, it can be a party bus howling downtown, or it can be a tearful bumpy ride in a harsh, dry desert. Life is never the same. So, should we start logging and analyzing each instance of experience? The answer is "No," it is a perfectly imperfect recipe of paralysis by analysis, state of mind. Whereas, the answer lies in abstracting the instances of experience to the level of its fertilizing ground and take it beyond.

The art of abstraction of objective experiences to their subjective level is the key to progress in self-inquiry. It requires to *witness* the subjective awareness and the lifecycle of objective expereince (physical and mental) as a *practical discipline* in human consciousness. Let's go a little further into it. Although everyone's graph of self-discovery is unique, still it can be abstracted in three simple, yet profound questions:

1. What is the real nature of my being?
2. What is the nature of becoming, because of my life experiences?
3. What is the nature of existence (beyond being and becoming), in which experiences occur?

Interestingly, the common denominator of these three questions is consciousness, which is the field of awareness in which human experiences are formed and felt. An analogy can be drawn between the light and consciousness. We see the world in the presence of light, but the light itself is not seen, as if it remains in our blind spot. Similarly, we experience everything in our consciousness but live oblivious of consciousness itself. Therefore, we require a special effort to understand the play of consciousness in our living experience. The reason for this special effort is not in the difficulty of realizing consciousness but the difficulty in clearing the clutter of content, which distorts the perception and hides clarity. For example, if you wish to cross a twenty-meter-long room, it may take a few seconds, but if the room is full of furniture, it will take special effort.

Thus, we need to prioritize to clear up the clutter for self-inquiry, it is not a thought experiment, but a practical philosophy to drive our efforts.

How do we de-clutter consciousness? Should we run away from life and people? Or, resist hard anything incoming into life by creating walls around us?

The answer i s "No," as Carl Jung said, "what you resist not only persists but will grow in size." On the contrary, we need to embrace and feel the experience, not as a consenting consumer, but watch with great awareness and discipline in our being, without creating permanent identity in us. Of course, record and respond the expereince, as needed. But, finally let it come and let it go. This discipline of action, can neither be delegated nor be postponed but can only be exercised in day to day life.

Unfortunately, in the popular human world, without this attitude of *witnessing* and *expanding* awareness, a being's identity is reduced into a resume of material ownerships. The question of identity is no longer *who am I?* Instead it is, *what I have?* Due to this distortion, the real being—as an existential fact, is forgotten; it has become fiction. Whereas, ego—a fictional identity, has become a driving factor of our living experience. Thus, it is reasonable to say that both the glory and the story of our existential identity, are severely depreciated.

Therefore, to regain the glory of being, we need to discriminate existential facts from worldly fiction at its root level. This requires a basic inquiry into the nature of being as an individual—a non-divisible ground being. In simple words, *who am I?* Also, this inquiry of being is intimately interwoven with the exploration of the nature of becoming. In simple words, *what is my story?* But, this inquiry of Being and Becoming will be incomplete and inaccurate without going beyond these two, into the ground of experience—consciousness.

Let's put these three—I, my story, and existential consciousness, under the lens of abstraction to understand the bigger picture, one by one. A little deliberation can reveal that exploration of being and becoming is two dimensional. One is worldly—made-up and utilitarian, and the other is existential—naturally manifested. Undoubtedly, these two dimensions are intertwined; they intersect and influence each other to make four coordinates of exploration.

First, *worldly-being* manifests as a made-up identity, for example, national, social, commercial, and so on. Second, *worldly-becoming* terms of success and failures defines our daily life. Third, *existential- being* manifested as our inner aliveness as a living species. Fourth, *existential-becoming* in terms of the human life cycle—birth, growth, reproduction, decay, and death. All these coordinates are common "known sources" of living experiences.

Because we must start from where we are, it is logical to first understand the *worldly-being and becoming*. Like any form of artificial arrangement, it has a contextual value, a structure, methods/ rules, tools, defined outcomes, and, most importantly, an identity. In this way, entire humanity is organized into small/ large scale *structures* —national, commercial, social and religious etc. these structures provide calculated *values*—security (physical or financial), importance, power, and so on. But there are defined *rules*, *tools* and *techniques* to derive these values, like—business, markets, society, parliaments, worship places. Accordingly, the ownership of earned values entitles the *identity* to you, in terms of—CEOs, Presidents, Gurus, Reformers, Priests etc. Largely, our understanding of existence is reduced to a level of a made-up world, as a big market, where our relationships are defined contractually, and we are commodities of calculated worth. This simulated life demands a mind full of desires and jealousy and is very stressful.

On other hand, *existential-being and becoming* is much more elaborate and sagacious than the worldly dimension. It becomes more subtle and mystical as we go deep inside our living framework. The pure being is innermost aliveness upon which our various bodies—physical, mental, and spiritual, are working. These are always in *becoming* mode—consciously or unconsciously. Since inception to expiration, we encounter experiences in terms of breathing, sleeping, dreaming, thinking, sensing, aging, health, sickness, pleasure, and so on. This inquiry is deep, delicate, and disciplined. It requires us to enhance awareness into the working of our *existential being and its becoming*. One key mantra is to experience directly the truth as it is. The direct realization cultivates a sense of meaningful contentment and joy in *being*; and it allows for an insight into the nature of *becoming*. One realizes that he/she does not become anything but is always becoming, thus one can let go of a made-up seperate identities; and enjoy being and becoming in cosmic togetherness. After gaining insight into existential-being and becoming, one can move beyond into the vast field of conciosuness as a background of these two, which also indicates formlessness.

In summary, going beyond these four object-oriented nodes into the ground of subjective awareness to realize our connection with existence is true self-inquiry. This realization results in unlocking the intrinsic joy of existence and keeps the human consciousness fresh and free of the burden of its content. The primary tool for this exploration is consciousness, and the primary result is also the transformation of consciousness.

For the same reason, this book is created with an intention to inspire the inquisitiveness of seekers, and steer the *seeking* towards the realization of three basic goals:

1. "Being," which is the unconditional self, subtler than the the made-up identity
2. "Becoming," which is the existential story of being, subtler than the autobiography
3. Moving "beyond" the being and the story of becoming

These three goals align with the title of this book—*being, becoming, and beyond.*

This book establishes that we are progenies of existential consciousness and not prototypes of an invented world. As a catalytic tool, this book will propel the self-exploration effort, while at the same time, helping to cut off ideological attachments and limitations.

Metaphorically, the reading experience can be summed up as one ground, one nail, one hammer, and twenty-one strokes. The ground is vast existence, the nail is awareness, the hammer is intention as its handle with effort as its head, and the twenty-one strokes are the topics in this book. Hit them hard, one by one, as needed. May you experience the joy of existential oneness!

The entire endeavor has been written in a simple and easily consumable format; where each topic is presented with sharp ideas, vivid imagery, poetry, and meaningful illustrations.

An important point to acknowledge is that this book may contain new and creative thoughts, but the essential spirit of expressions scribed in it is ancient and unchanged. Perhaps everything said here is already spoken but with a different style and perspective.

Another point to mention is that all the chapters presented in this book, including the cover page, start with the words "O Beloved," which signify my sincere heartfelt desire to connect the reader with a feeling of love and trust, more than any philosophy or artwork. I believe, without this feeling, any form of conversation is meaningless.

The main body of this book offers four sections containing twenty- one independent chapters. Each chapter has its independent core message and begins with a *Prelude* to provide perspective. The chapters are organized into sections to group similar ideas together for the sake of retaining focus while reading. However, each chapter has its individual core message and can be read on its own, anytime.

The four sections are as follows:

1. *The Glory of Being* reflects upon various aspects of unconditional identity. The key message is to polish the *being* enough to shine as a pure individual.

2. *Harmony in Becoming* establishes that becoming is a foundational principle of nature, and its realization is of supreme relevance. Additionally, this section depicts the popular meaning of becoming and its ailments versus existential becoming and its supplements.

3. *Moving Beyond* prepares and orients oneself for practical meditative action to explore the existential truth beyond the being and becoming. It also elaborates upon the type of attitudes one must attain for self-exploration.

4. *Four-Step Meditation Technique* is a bonus section, codified in textbook style. It provides practical methods of mindfulness meditation in a very crisp, clear, and concise manner.

Thereupon, this book ends with a short concluding note and a glossary to explain the uncommon or non-english words.

One may ask, "Who should read it?" or "How should someone read it?" The answer is simple and natural. This work is for all curious human beings, regardless of age, gender, nationality, class, color, or education. However, it will benefit readers differently. Primarily, three types of people will find it more interesting. First, someone who is already working sincerely on self-exploration will find it most useful. Second, a person who is curious and determined to look inward will find many solutions in it. Third, a person who has a dormant curiosity dumped under social dust will find it inspiring to jump above these hurdles. In short, this work intends to create questions for sleepwalkers, answers for the curious souls, assurance for the conscious explorers, and above all, motivation for all *beings*.

Read the poem—*A Brief Note to Readers* before starting to read the book. The best way to read it is not to read just as a reader but as an author yourself. Read, reflect, and author your conclusions and create your vision. Thereupon, validate your conclusions, repeat the cycle, and revise your conclusions until you touch the existential connection.

Now, are you ready for the play of consciousness? Are you ready to grow out of your old ways?

If the answer to either of these questions is "yes," then this is the greatest moment of your life because no matter how long the journey is; it always starts with the first step in the right direction.

As Gautama Buddha said, "There are only two mistakes one does on the path to liberation: first by not starting it and second by not finishing it." So, go on.

A Note to Readers

O Beloved Reader,
in this world of countless complexions don't you desire your
original reflection?

    Here is a book that is your tool,
    but before you read it, know some of the rules.

Sip before you drink and taste before you eat;
don't be in a hurry to gulp, as this is your lover's treat.

    Read aloud from your mouth and listen from your ears
    with an alert mind, a receptive heart, and a face full of
    cheers.

Read it slow and let it flow
in the soil of your heart, let it grow.

    There are twenty-one seeds with germs of wisdom,
    countless would-be the flowers, blooming out of them.

Spraying on you, the sweet perfume of love,
thus silently, snug inside you, like a hand in a glove.

    It is informational, and it is aspirational,
    it is emotional, and it is sensational.

Somewhere it is deep, and somewhere it is high; somewhere it is
juicy, and somewhere it is dry.

    Just like your life, it has many flavors,
    but unless you work upon it, it won't do any favors.

Though the intent is to simplify
the wisdom of sages into a lullaby.

    But you need to consume it, and you need to apply
    no magic! But your own steps will raise the ladder in
    the sky.

Read wholeheartedly and reflect,

and use "your" reasoning to connect.

  Remember always, no work of words can be invigorating;

  words are only pointers; your own experience is liberating.

From the pen of an ordinary *being*

it is written and with a sincere heart and deep thinking.

  To open the doors of "existential kingdom,"

  O Beloved, it is a gift to you, out of my love, and out my wisdom.

Section 1

The Glory of Being

Can there be a world without doors of eyes,
nose, ears, skin, and tongue?
Can you see, smell, hear, touch, and taste without mind?
Can your mind perceive without you?
Then, who are you?
Discover your original ID card—an unedited version.

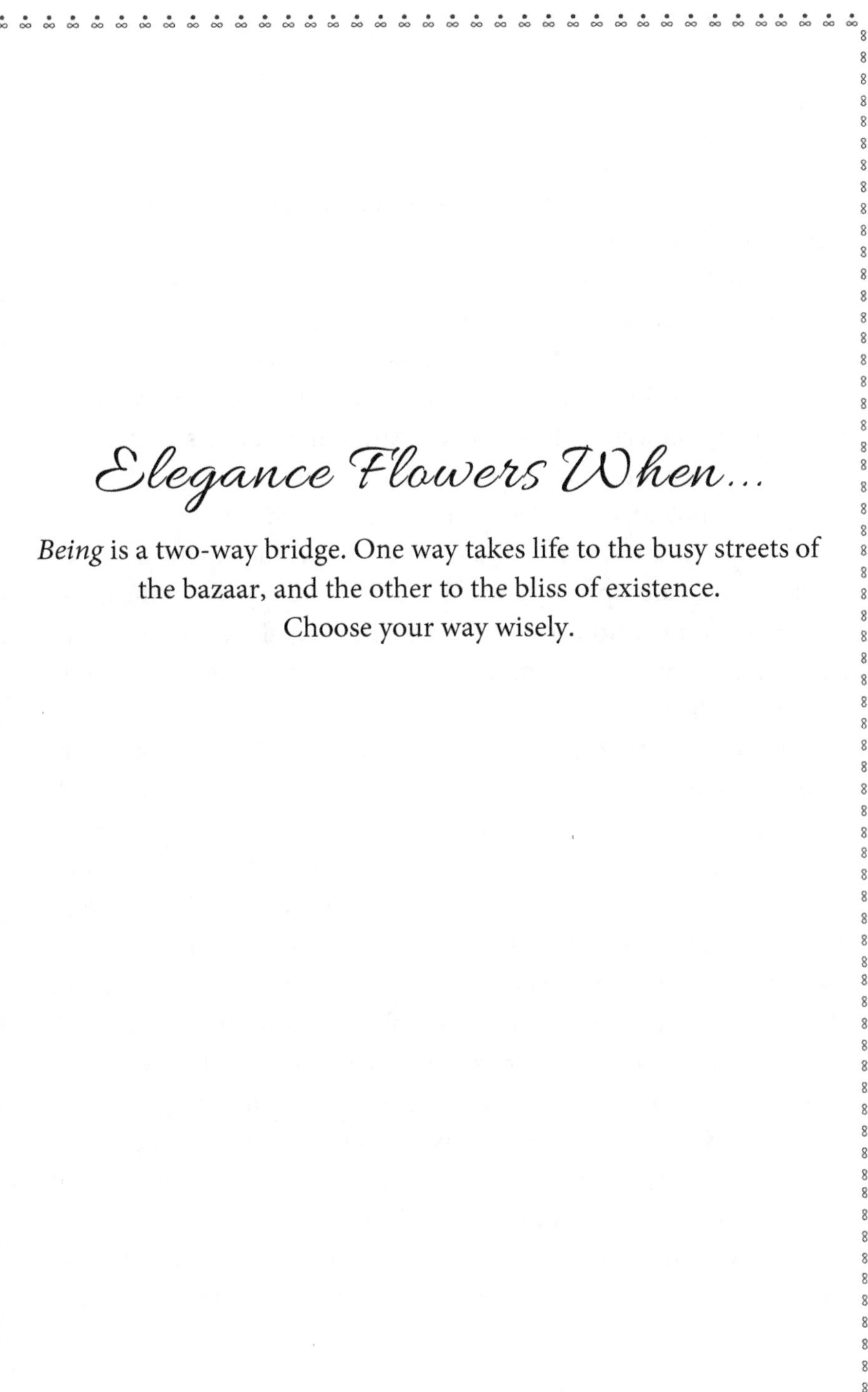

Elegance Flowers When...

Being is a two-way bridge. One way takes life to the busy streets of the bazaar, and the other to the bliss of existence.
Choose your way wisely.

Prelude

In one way, the *being* can be described as our innermost aliveness and animating life force acting as a foundation of our mind-matter framework. To understand it, close your eyes, invert awareness deep inside you, feel, and connect to your inner aliveness. This sense and assertion of your aliveness is your living *being*.

When an individual *being* attains existential grace, he or she feels rooted in the ground of existential reality. A deep sense of meaningful connection to all arises. Attainment of this elegance is the taste of existential joy and wisdom, which naturally flowers from within. It is not borrowed from the extraneous material world.

On the contrary, our everyday reality is occupied in the invented goals of this made-up world, which we think we enjoy—in the name of success, competition, groupism, power, inequality, and so on. We end up assuming and accepting this made-up design as a default way of living in the world.

It is evident that, as per this world design, the individuals are tailoring their lives to match the outer expectations, and they push themselves into a daily mill. Evidently, everyone is motivated to comply and compete within social norms for a better livelihood, resulting in a stressful living experience. Interestingly, the endorsed escape mechanisms from this stress and suffering are also cut from the same cloth, in the form of entertainment, games, media, rituals, clubs, and so on. Hence both the problems and solutions are made out of the same mindset. For example, if an individual suffers from social politics and pressures, then popular solutions are going to a pub, a movie, a game, a yoga class, or so on. These are common bandages. And, when the old bandage become limitations, we invent new adjustments, but out of the same old mindset.

Consequently, life gets transformed into a circular maze. At best, we relieve ourselves by using temporary bandages and tranquilizers.

This is the same for the large scale as well. For example, we (*as a human race*) have invented the geographical organizations in the world in the form of nations, evolved out of tribes and territories. And, because we are afraid of each other, we have invented arms and armies as security measures along with our territories. Simultaneously, to reduce tension, we developed treaties, ties, and trusted contracts to manage territorial interests. Of course, we have not created these arrangements to secure us from some aliens or other species, but from other humans. In other words, so much of human energy and investments are going into managing the fear and distrust among ourselves. And, we fail to eradicate and evolve out of the fear of each other; instead, we choose to live and manage it with sub-optimal arrangements. It is just one example out of hundreds, we see in our everyday lives as human beings.

Thus, at both individual and collective social levels, we have bandages and workarounds designed for our made-up world limitations.

One continues to live divided and broken until one day he or she gets tired of it and says enough is enough—I must find a way out of this rut, and realize the truth of my existential root. Thereupon, one instantly realizes that the very next thing is to inquire how one's mind got into this trap and remained in its clutch. This diagnosis is a fundamental step forward.

One futuristic dream is that humanity is designed to transmit human values in such a way that when a child is born, the culture itself promotes the *existential intelligence* rather than localized intellectual designs and divisions. So, we understand real belongingness to existence rather than living by relationships based on conditions. (For more on it, read the poem **"Life Together"** in section#2).

In short, human life is a rare event and is meant to be lived with joy and grace. Let this life be not used up in imposed ideas of a made-up world. Rather, devote this event in the realization of your *being's* originality and its relationship as a primary agenda. Consequently, when a *being* awakens, his or her life experience is nothing short of cosmic elegance and lives an easy and effortless life based on existential awareness.

This poem portrays the qualitative expressions of a liberated *being* who lives a life aligned to the real and ordinary existence, infinite and available. It embraces the elegance and excellence of life and attempts to sketch the glory of real *being*. Further, it elaborates on the flowering of *being* up to existential levels and the attributes of conscious living.

The best way to read it is to feel its meaning in life, instead of intellectualizing it. Read it slow and relate the situations of life to when you felt this way, taking this poem as a mirror.

Poem

OBeloved,
when the elegance touches
the fibers of soul,
the being feels ONE
with the existence as a whole.

begets the love,
begets the wisdom,
with the warmth of oneness
in the womb of freedom.

Excellence fills the life
to the brim.
Contentment and gratitude
become the favorite hymn.

The *Being* reforms into an incense of elegance
where the dialects of life are no more opposite,
and polarization occurs
only to deposit.

Thereupon, one never feels lonely,
yet is always alone.
Lives without any best friend
and the enmity is far gone.

With a serious mind
and a humorous heart
enjoy togetherness,
and wish, to (*in relation*) never depart.

Prefers to trust
than to doubt.
Offers silence in strife
than to shout.

Dislikes laziness
and dislikes any addiction,
but a heart full of vigor
with thy benediction.

Always busy,
with something to attend,
but remains easy
as no fear of the end.

Feels life,
rather than think about it.
Examines thyself,
rather to blink about it.

Simplicity shines
in the harmony of three:
Intention, Word, and Action are one,
to fulfill with joy and lives gap-free.

O Beloved,
It's worth exploring the beauty of elegance.
Let the elegance flower in your *being* and
shine as the beauty of thine.

The Grain, Dunes of Desert and My Reminiscences

(I > we, where "we" is a created class)

Prelude

This poem is a song and a scream of your soul.

The moment we are born, we are already classified. The human being is not valued by virtue of being *human*, but by the rules created by society. Your value is assessed by wealth, color, caste, creed, language, social status, nationality, religion, and so on. The worldly arrangements are designed in such a way that, even though they are temporary and superimposed on us, they are considered more valuable than the individual human. Thus, to be valued and accepted in society, we are forced to look out into the world to compete for extrinsic values, and deprioritize our efforts to look inward to our innate value. Some societies may claim to be more mindful in cherishing individuality, but differences are superficial and in degrees only. The result is obvious; we forget our soul and accept a social-psychological Ego complex as our ground-self. Consequently, human being's understanding of real self-hood has become too shallow. (Read poem **"Ego"** for more on it). This basis of living is forged and causing illusory problems in society, although the effect can be real on individuals. For example, some people are made to believe that they are inferior due to status, gender, language, or color, etc. and suffer in silence. It's like when fear in a dream can make you sweat in real life.

If you compare the world with a vast desert and zoom in, you will find that classes, castes, creeds, nations, tribes, and religions are like dunes in deserts. These societal dunes are formations of grains— *individual beings*, acted upon by cultures like winds, make dunes in the desert. The odd shapes of dunes are like inequalities in the social world, where one is higher or lower in their relationships work "with another." Their shapes look strong and permanent but are conditional and impermanent; thus, these are *untrue* existentially. Only grains—individual beings, hold the truth. Thus, the immense disparity in the world is a myth, an outcome of a human-made design, and the social reforms to counter it, to bring equality is another myth. The actual truth is in individuality. Hence every individual being must be valued as an expression of existence.

Let's go deeper. We associate and conform to various socio-economic-religious forms, and assume a personality limited by the perimeters of respective classification, and we end up becoming a puppet of a fictional world, living under the weight of its belief system. Illusions of the world are readily accepted as reality with a conformist mindset. Therefore, the individuality remains hidden in the terms and conditions of the agreeable widespread slavery of classifications.

If you place a big sieve under the dunes of the desert and let the dunes slip through it, you will realize the actuality of the grains. Similarly, if you cut down all the classifications and conditioning, you will attain a fresh outlook for humanity, and see a human being as a real individual grain born out of existential reality. And, you will connect to the person behind personality, be it a connection to yourself or the other *being*.

Being an individual is the truth of existence; thus, individuality is the plug into existential reality. Anyone serious about realizing the truth of *being* and its relationship to the existence must strive to realize his or her indivisible self. Understanding individuality both at thinking and experiencing level is the primary step towards exploring consciousness and real transformation.

Humanity should embrace it, and human beings should be nurtured to explore their aboriginal identity and relationship to real existence rather than being morphed into classes and levels.

A human being is a beautiful creation of existence, and to be born as a human is enough on its own to be valued, and the human-made worldly formations are merely supporting reasons for the convenient sustenance of humanity.

This poem cherishes the idea that individuality is a greater strength than the formations in the world. Individuality is the existential reality, and establishments are merely imposed reality.

A word of caution is that this poem is not an attempt in any way to critically examine the socio-political theories of *Collectivism vs. Individualism*. The reader is advised not to get entangled into comparisons of political philosophies through this poem. Instead, this is purely written to shift the perceptual gear inwardly with a much more profound goal to inquire oneself and the layers of conditional personality, which prohibits us from realizing the true "self." The spotlight is on "YOU" as an individual (*indivisible self*) and not you vs. the other. Therefore, this poem is not examining theories of selfishness, individualism, or collectivism, as many of the world philosophers have talked about.

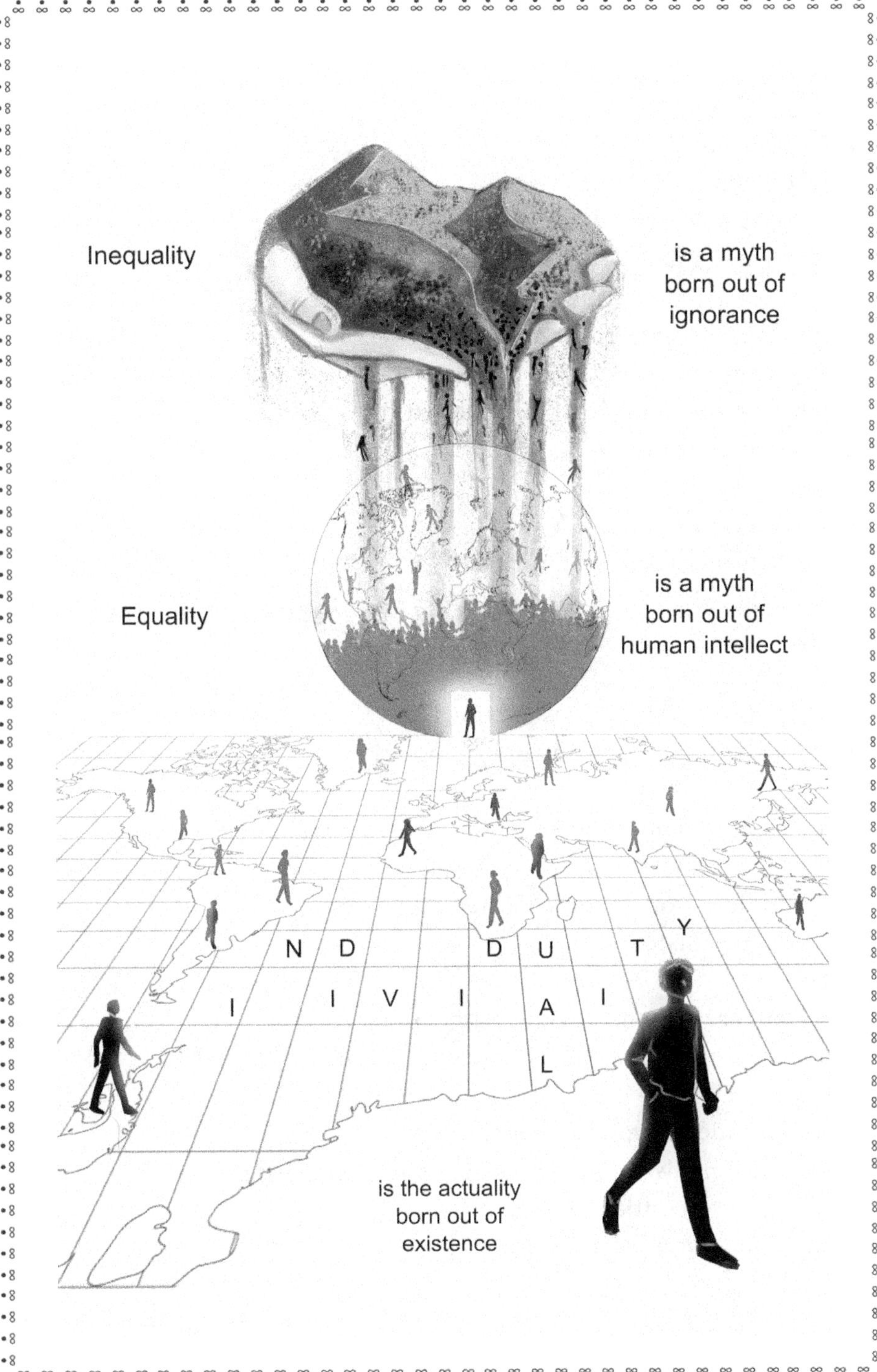

Inequality
is a myth
born out of
ignorance
Equality
is a myth
born out of
human intellect
INDIVIDUAL DUTY
is the actuality
born out of
existence

Poem

OBeloved,
do not ask me, the age
of my life. Ask me how many lives
I have lived in this age.

I have lived here much before the birth
of my memory.
I have suffered here much before the birth
of my known agony.

I traveled here
much before my known journeys.
I dwelled here
much before the known colonies.

Yet you lose me in your fascinations.
And, yet, you refuse me in your dominations.

You run out, to be designed in an earthly template
and grind and sweat yourself to be elaborate.
I wonder how you miss me? When I am your
inmost immediate.

Alas! you are poisoned by the magic of many
And confused by the traffic of plenty.

Thus, bewildered, you run helter-skelter.
Now stop! and listen, I am your soul, your seamless shelter.
Don't be shy to settle in me,
because no one else can set you free.

I am the One where the silence flows.
I am the One who truly knows.
I am the One in which things appear.
And I am the One untouched by fear.

I am *the unity*, and I am You.
Know that behind the clouds, you are blue.
Live high and live deep. You are the existence!
Look and leap.

O Beloved, do not ask the desert,
"How many dunes do you have?"
Do not ask the dunes,
"How many grains do you have?"
Ask the grain,

"How many dunes have you seen?"
Because these dunes and deserts
merely exist in your imposed reality,
but the grain persists in its own
composed actuality.

When the world got shrunk till unity,
and the unity sprung out beyond eternity.
At this very moment, appears the *being* as a bridge to beyond.
Thus, sieve the deserts and dunes to free the grain,
and commune only to nourish and not to reign.

O Beloved, may every grain gain
grace by realizing their indigenous vitality
and be saved from becoming
a thing in the world of inflicted reality.

Sparkling Stars, I Wonder Who Created Them

Great news! You, as a pure *Being*, and Existence are one.

Prelude

"Tat Tvam Asi" is a significant announcement recorded in *Chandogya Upanishad* by the ancient sages of India. It simply means "you are that." It is the highest level of *being*'s glorification ever stated. It means that you are identical with the ultimate reality, out of which all existence has been manifested. Our pure spirit, or true identity, is as vast as the sky and wants to breathe open, and live unbound.

On the contrary, the understanding of our self is greatly edited by our education, teaching, and parenting systems.

The direct realization of this shorthanded version of self, and removal of its conditionality, is the prerequisite to uncover our real identity and its relationship to existence. Also, this discovery need not be a crazy social journey and fight with everything around, but a mindful personal endeavor. It is not a public affair. The primary reason to commit self-inquiry deeply into the core of our *being* is to glorify human consciousness to existential levels. It allows us to realize that we are the co-creator of existence and do not have a separate self.

This poem motivates the human spirit towards the higher consciousness, where it has no separate identity from cosmic existence. After reading it, close your eyes and say in your heart, "Tat Tvam Asi, I am that—One with existence."

Poem

OBeloved,
On that clear night in the harsh summer of June, it was a bit cooler, and, hiding from all, I escaped from my mundane cocoon.

And I found for myself a vast open ground, where I rested, to gaze upon the stars, sky, and the silence around.

It echoed in my heart, "What divides me from the infinite, and what settles the noises into the quiet?"

Thereupon happened a magic that my spirit reflected onto the vast black sky and was hanging on the firmament, like a night fly, as if it belongs to the infinite silence, and in this way, uttered its ultimate essence.

Asked my baffled mind to the shining spirit in the sky,

"Who has sprinkled the glittering stars in the night, riding the ship of clouds in this oceanic sky, and secreting the pulsating secrets of existence?"

Replied my spirit,

"I wonder if I did it when I was fully awake before I slept in this life after drinking the wine of names, forms, and meanings, soaked in the knowledge of this world."

This prolonged dream about "Me" has grown so deep, along with the roots of my beingness, that the "Self" forgot its nature, aboriginal.

And, I would have slept for eternity unless a merciful spark of pure but latent "Self" alarmed me that I was asleep fast.

This alarm was very troublesome but intensely wise, as I knew *now* is the time to wake up and leave the futile games of this raw flesh and stale mind.

Just beware! Not to snooze on this call for the comfort of sleep.

For the first time, I realized that this real treasure of mine is so tired of this thick and dusty worldly hangover.

And I wish to be awakened again to bathe in the fresh fountain of life and play with these sparkling stars and live forever.

I wish to remain in my original essence, as it is now and was before when I was split into space and time and accepted this incarnation evolved out of traditions.

I don't have any answers to share, but I know how to put the questions to bed. I don't have any knowledge to reconcile divisions of the world, but I know the wisdom of oneness in existence.

O Beloved, let the *being* be fully awakened and out of the comforts of sleep, and let it live by the purity of its source and essence.

Ego, The Relationship Insulator

Ego makes many heads in you, but conceals your real one.

Prelude

The ego plays a significant role in our psychological operating system. It creates a sense of entitlement for our everyday experiences—intended, imposed, or imagined. It's an outer substitute for our unknowable inner sense of self, in our known language. It is supported by mental objects— thoughts, emotions, concepts, images, expectations, memories, and so on; arising and vanishing in our consciousness. And, its strength is situational; it varies by the grip of these objects. For example, the ego is reduced in deep meditative states or sleep, and enhanced in strong competitive arguments.

Let's go a little deeper into its functioning, roots, and results.

Over time, a *being* passes through many experiences. Each experience stores its sensations and their associated mental images made of perceptions, actions, thoughts, and feelings. Mostly, these experiences are goal-oriented, comparative, and competitive. Therefore, our self-image is a complex calculation of several ideas made out of a divided world-image, in terms of "me vs. you." This self-image, commonly called as ego, is a deeply rooted psychological complex, expressing itself as a superior or inferior *being*, upon worldly interaction. It acts as a command center, and a reference point in our consciousness, and guides our attitudes—attachments, aversions, and the value system.

This superior or inferior ego-complex is fundamentally interested in self-importance. Therefore, it is always judgmental, stubborn, and selfish. A mindless attachment to this self-image makes our psyche shortsighted about the other human beings and cosmic existence. Therefore, an egoistic mind has a strong habit pattern and an enhanced tendency to ignore the existential reality.

The fundamental problem of an egoistic mind is that it creates psychological insulation for any meaningful connection to other *beings* and oneself. It does not matter if we feel superior or inferior; in both cases, we fail to connect. Due to this psychological glitch, human beings live as isolated islands in vast existential ocean and create suffering for each other."

In short, the ego is a relationship insulator. Unfortunately, most of us connect with each other via our ego-adapters only. As a result, we live insulated existentially, but plug-in socially through adapters of traditions, roles, rituals, economic needs, religions, groups, languages, and so on. Invariably, these adapters may work in one situation and fail in others.

Why is it important to talk here?

For a *being* on the path of self-exploration, the ego is a tremendous block. Hence understanding it, and melting this hindrance away is the key to make any meaningful progress.

The truth is that a *being* is fundamentally a non-entity and an ego- less state. Whereas, the ego is not an existential reality. It's a fiction but appears real because of the continuous sense of identification and ownership during an experience. Continuity and lack of self-awareness create the illusion of a permanent entity.

Let's understand it using an analogy. Suppose in a dark room, on a moving conveyor belt, there are chocolate pieces placed at equal distance. These pieces fall into a bin at the end of the belt, one after another, as the belt moves. Now take a torch with a sharp beam of light and point it on the endpoint from where the chocolate pieces fall off. Switch on exactly at the time when a chocolate piece arrives at the endpoint and switch off right after it. If you switch on and off the torch at the same frequency as the speed of the belt, then to an ignorant person, it will appear that the chocolate piece is always present and permanently located even though the truth is that it is a series of chocolate pieces moving on continuously. To remove this misperception, you have to switch on the lights in the room so that the entire game is seen.

Likewise, the ego (as a chocolate piece) is a psychological sense, lives as part and parcel of every passing experience, just appears to be permanent because our awareness of experience is very limited.

The result is that we stitch our personal suit (*ego*) for our *Self* and hide it behind the ego. Then, we live insulated from the rest of our existence. But, if you switch on the light of self-awareness, you can see a series of mental objects (thoughts, feelings, and emotions, etc.) passing through in an experience, but no permanent ego. Indeed, it is also impermanent, like any other experience.

Now, the key question arises, if the ego is a non-existential fiction and makes us an ignorant *being*, how can we melt away its insulator-effect? Thereupon, how can we develop existential connectivity?

In many groups or societies, it is commonly suggested to suppress the ego by putting effort into becoming humble, apologetic, or even suffer pain as an antidote. But, one must know that suppression is violence towards oneself, and apologies create guilt in oneself. Efforts like these create another image of the ego. An illusion cannot be eradicated by any coercive effort, but only by awakening to it, by acute awareness.

Therefore, to bypass the ego, it is primary to understand its rising, sustaining, and dying. Any time a self-image is created and felt in mind, one needs to be aware of it, and let it go as the related thought or action, dies out. This way, the *being* remains empty of attachment of any self-image as a permanent entity. Consequently, one can live free of ego and full of wisdom, thus cultivates compassion. For a mindful *being*, the ego is a psychological plastic, hence required to be carefully examined, and flushed out. This ego-free mind gives the space to deeper states of experiences, which are more fulfilling and meaningful.

Another essential point to understand is the difference between ego and individuality. Ego is comparative, whereas *individuality* is pure self, not against anyone. Secondly, the ego is a crowded self-image, whereas *individuality* is indivisibility.

This poem is a short exploration of the ego and its functions. It also sketches the state of a *being* whose actions are results of knowing and awareness of a situation, rather than a preconceived solid self-image as the center of activity.

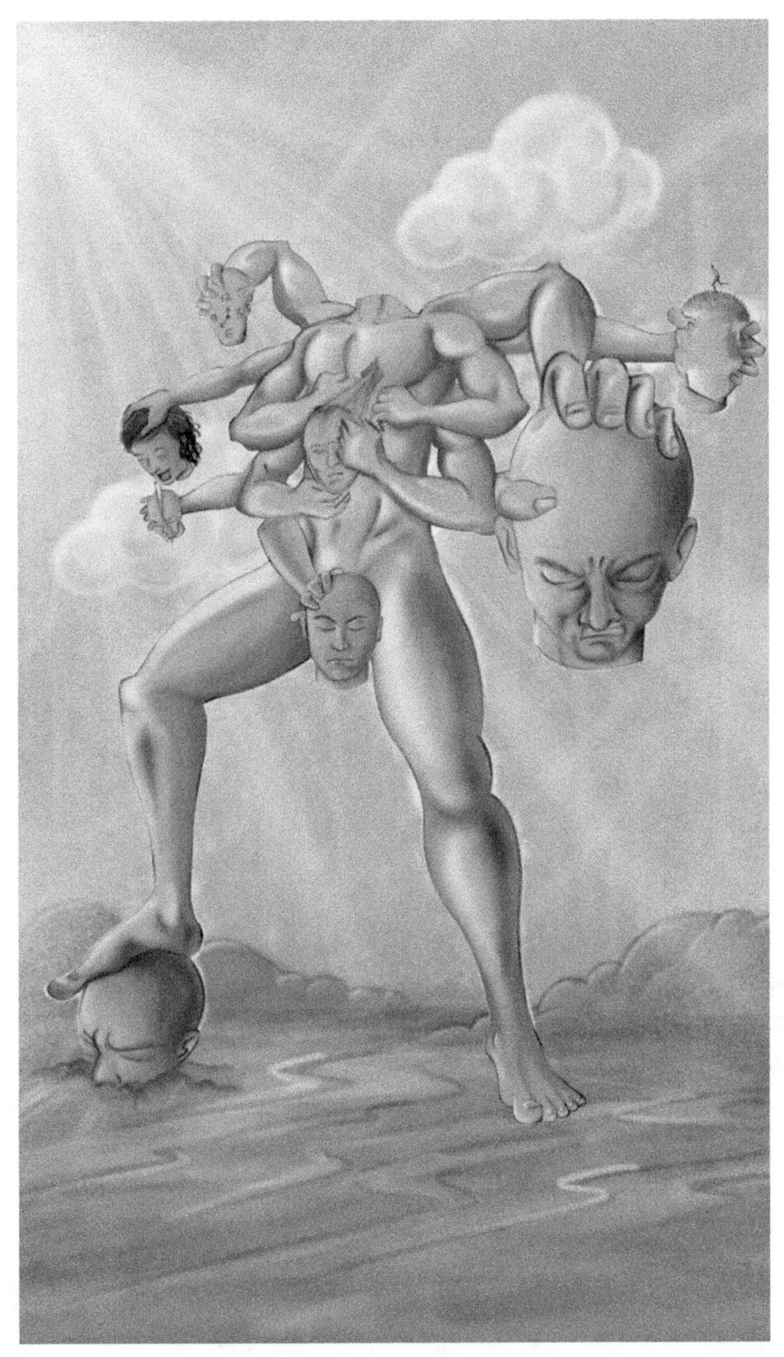

Poem

OBeloved,
the way in which this "I" germinates,
the way in which this "I" exterminates,
is a way, no doubt,
but not "the way out."

To the unclear mind,
this "I" lives and dies as an impulsive wave
to project itself on the mind
and hide in an unknown cave.

The *being* does not see it
and its—how, when, and where?
Because the natural habit of mind
is to natively adhere.

This compulsive adherence
brings forth the identification,
and superimposes the experiences on the mind
in several layers of "mentation."

The identification and mentation together
conceives a sense of self,
thereupon, this sense gets detached
from others and lives in its own, private cell.

This very cell on its own
could not realize its mother,
and while swimming in the social life
brings friction with the other.

This friction and gap
deteriorates humankind,
and thus, motivates the wise
to explore their *Mind*.

O Beloved wise explorer,
be the truth and be its bearer,
trust your empirical insight,
by witnessing ego in your own light.

With full energy and attention,
attend the "I" and its conception,
observe its birth, movement, and death
to have clear insight while moving the breath.

Focus awareness on the evolution of thought
and impel no effort, either to decorate or to distort.
Just watch unbiased, and let it reveal,
the play of ego and its manipulative deal.

Know its very life and resurrection.
Let the wisdom taste this action,
one at a time but in every action,
and then be a distant *witness of action* per action.

Does it exist independent of thought?
Does it change its weight based on the lot?
Do emotions color it by strokes of memories?
Does it change with love, loneliness, or broken worries?

When is it strong, and when is it weak?
When does it occur more? In waking, dream, or sleep?
When does the mind encounter its deepest invasion?
When it lives alone or lives by worldly comparison?

The warmth of this insight
has a majestic essence.
It melts the mountain of identity
with its very presence.

It perfumes your life as never before,
and ego no longer defines your living shores,
although it remains a benign activity of the core,
but it does not endure in you or me anymore.

Life flows together as a Great Integrity.
The self exists with the action, merely *To-Be*,
not fixed in the significance of its content.
And ego is operative merely as a signature of intent.

This so-called *self* becomes an empty drum.
What music will flow through it?
Is dependent on the hand,
be it sweet or be it a strum.

This emptiness brings
a beautiful uncertainty,
which is only one side of the coin
and the other is creativity.

Should the knower of this be anything?
Or, should the knower of this be nothing?
Or live carefree of *be* or *not-to-be*?
Better to live choiceless than to agree.

Oneness of *be* and *be-not* completes the circle of awareness,
not-knowing to knowing to empty-unknown.
This "I" came from nowhere to me
And I do not know where it has gone.

The glorified drop,
who lives in sweet devotion,
understands the oneness of all
knows the taste of the ocean.

O Beloved,
Bless the *being*
with the wisdom of the snake,
who will shed the skin easily,
when it outgrows its old make.

Let the cognizance outgrow the self-knowledge
to shed the ego painlessly and free itself from its cage.
Thereupon, one lives humble at heart and enlightened in mind,
life becomes a joyful journey instead of a wasteful grind.

Blessed Sufferer

Dukkha, Samudaya, Nirodha, and Magga.
There is suffering, it has an origin, it can be ceased,
and the means—to terminate it.

- The four noble truths, Buddha

Prelude

While waking up in the morning, pinch your elbow hard. You will notice that the awareness which was freely moving in the body has been imprisoned by the pain and collected in your elbow. The pain has a distinct quality of binding human consciousness towards itself. And when this pain becomes chronic, it transforms into suffering.

Human beings suffer from either physical or mental pain every day. Thus, the awareness lives in the bondage of suffering. In this way, the free awareness of life is narrowed down and collected in daily living due to suffering in life. In response to it, we all try to get rid of suffering as soon as possible, but we do not want to be aware of its roots. We all worry about the suffering and objects attached to suffering, but we rarely put effort into exploring the nature of suffering itself. Thus, we almost always manage it superficially by controlling extraneous factors.

Suffering causes deep internal bondage and a burden on the *being*. It is much deeper than the pain. In pain, people—fight, flight, or freeze as an immediate response. Whereas suffering is chronic, and if it becomes intense, it sucks all the energy. Commonly, there are only two doors left for a suffering soul: hope or hide. Thus, if some energy is left, then   the *being* hopes for the best to occur, else gives up and hideaway.

This poem points towards a third door—heedfulness of suffering. It's not about doing anything about suffering in terms of hope or hiding away but to be aware of the nature of suffering in its entirety— symptoms, diagnosis, prognosis, and treatment, as said in four noble truths by Buddha.

Direct awareness of suffering is itself a healer and will cut out the roots of it. It can help in creating a beautiful experience beyond suffering.

Poem

O Beloved,
When the life moves into a thin alley, and nothing it holds
but a shivering belly, the whole action it can take is to stand by.
As it has neither the energy to fight nor desire to fly.

When the rigid pain has melted itself into suffering, and the flood
of feelings is filled with its sting,
the emotions effuse with the aimless motion, and the weary mind
needs just an explosion.

And the suffering stands with legs apart at your door, and whether
it brings in life or death, you don't care anymore.

And the teachings of hope and peaching horoscope burdens the
mind like a meaningless stale joke.

When the eyes doubt tears, and lose their shine, upon waiting
endlessly, imprisoned by the time.

O Beloved, that very moment,
Be immensely watchful, as this is a magical sign, and movement
through this pain is a play of thine.

There is nothing more left to lose, but only to gain. It is not another
"hope" but something more solid, though it appears insane.
Patience is the key, and aggression is a taboo because the door of
beingness has three ways, and the third is just above the two.

The third door opens, when the *being* cooperates, neither in life nor death and looks within, at this very moment, the universe of discreet living things transforms into connected *beings*.

Things have no meaning of their own, and beingness is a luminosity. Things live and die in suffering, and *being* has the taste of immortality.

O Beloved,
bestow the patience, and inwardness to the silent sufferers of this world.

Salvation

Asato ma sadgamya, Tamso Ma Jyotirgamya,
mritur ma amritamgamya.
Lead me:
from illusion to reality,
from darkness to light,
and from mortality to immortality.

-Brihadaranyaka Upanishad

Prelude

When you throw a stone in the sky, it falls back on earth. This happens due to the gravitational force of the earth, which resists the stone to keep going up. But, if the stone is thrown with such a massive force that it overcomes the resistance and never falls back, then this minimum velocity is called escape velocity. We can draw an interesting parallel in life science with these two terms—resistance and escape velocity.

Human beings are the most intelligent species, evident by their achievements and advancements on earth. Despite this, humanity suffers so much violence, poverty, social stress, suicide, competition, hatred, jealousy, and many more hardships.

Here, the term "suffering" is used for psychological suffering, which is different from physical pain, though it can be inter-related in its effect. For example, I have a headache, which is physical pain, and I start wondering, why me? What is the reason for my headache? Who is behind it? How can I take revenge? And so on, and build a story of suffering on top of it.

Why is human society not able to escape from suffering? It does not seem like the problems are due to natural resources, rather due to a social mindset which uses them. The way social issues are taking over our happiness, it feels like most of our psychological suffering is by design. And, if it is by design, it can be re-designed and aligned to the existential nature, which is far more intelligent than human intellect.

Everybody intrinsically desires freedom from suffering and live a happy life. However, only a few intend to look into this problem deeply, at a level of daily living experience. And, very rare and fortunate are those who courageously act upon to escape out of this bondage.

A few basic questions arise: What is this force of suffering? Why does it exist and endure? How can I escape out of this suffering? And, what is the minimum work required to escape the suffering?

It will be the most fruitful self-examination in life. No one will ever fail this exam; it can only bring progressive happiness and liberation at the end.

A mindless but common assumption we make is that our suffering is due to extraneous factors; whereas, the reality, rarely realized is that we cultivate its roots inside us with our own hands. For the same reason, its weeds can be uprooted from within using our own hands.

Self-concern and self-care are the primary virtues that collect the energy to weed out the roots and control conditions that allow one to suffer. This is the minimum energy needed to escape.

In this way, spirituality can be defined as the development of the spirit. In other words, to develop the spirit—pure and light, one must remove the root cause of suffering, consequently allowing the spirit to attain salvation. Liberation lives next door to the one who decides to come out of this inertia of suffering.

There can be several practical processes to develop the spirit; for example, devotion, yoga, methods of inquiry, and meditations, but the goal remains the same.

It is a short poem that elaborates on the burden of spirit, the prerequisite to unburden it, and an indication of a way to unburden it.

Poem

O Beloved,
look around, mostly we all are seeking two things:
to win over our desires, and to be saved from suffering.
So, shouldn't we realize first, our relationship to these
before jumping to learn liberation, from the typical theories?

Isn't knowing the formation of "self" a prerequisite for
transformation? And, isn't knowing the bondage of "self" a
prerequisite for liberation? Isn't the effort to know our bondages
more practical?
Isn't reading the given solutions, merely fictional?

If so, then let us be aware of bondage,
which is real and near to you,
And park aside all that,
whatever is elusive and unclear to you.

For this, one needs to be interested in and committed to oneself.
And, a deep sense of love and care, is to be cultivated for oneself.

Look carefully, in your life,
What makes you worry, in day or night? What makes your breath,
heavy or light? What makes your spirit, low or high?
What makes your heart sink, or fly?

Watch the moments closely,
when do you feel happy with anything or anyone?
And, when do you feel unhappy with anything or anyone?
When do you desire to attach with anything or anyone?
And, when do you desire to detach with anything or anyone?

Know these feelings and desires and the objects behind.
Go deep inside you, into their roots, to uncurl and unwind.
Why do you hold their burden on your "self," to begin with?
And ask, is it a real belonging of your "self," or a borrowed myth?

Sensibly, scan the stickers of your suffering,
and go deeper than the labels- into their making.
And, observe, what creates their glue in you,
which keeps these sufferings to continue in you.

Get engaged within yourself, and study very hard,
the relationship between your *being* and your I.D. card. And, also
between your personality and outer society, in the making up of
your daily life, and your life story.

Go even deeper than personality, to enquire,
into your ground *being*, and feel your pure desire.
Isn't it a feeling to live unblocked and free,
and perhaps it is the ONLY feeling that makes you happy.

On the contrary, go to the other side.
Now, do you see that the social world is designed to conform?
And, engaging mindlessly in it, causes your free spirit to deform.
This causes tension, because, internally you want to be free,
but, the world's entire learning convinces you, you can't be.

To ease the tension, you find countless cunning ways,
thus, become an expert in managing, inner, and outer maze.
In this struggle, your spirit forgets the real taste of freedom,
lives tired, confused, and unfulfilled under the social burden.

So, the social world has its own definition of freedom,
i.e., the capability to express and execute the desires of the forms.
Therefore, there is competition to maximize—power and choices,
without wondering, is it truly by winning a "choice" your "life" rejoices?

O Beloved, then what is true freedom?
Is it dependent on anything?
Or is it the opposite of any discipline?
Or is it having choices, always be available?
Or is it having the power, making you able?

Can it be attained by rage or revolt?
Can it be attained by becoming bold?
Can it be attained by hiding in a cave?
Can it be attained by sweating to be saved?

Now think upon these things:
Is it not undoing, whatever is done to you?
Is it not uncoiling, whatever is coiled in you?
Is it not freeing up, whatever is fixed in you?
Is it not making alive, whatever is dead in you?

O Beloved, know this clearly:
One may play with borrowed myths, only, until a moment arrives,
when he gains insight, by going behind the desires, into his real drives.
Thereupon, one lives fulfilled, when the real hunger of spirit is truly fed.
Until then, he can't be called living; at best, we can say: he is not dead.

Because, without this insight, the sheepish greed for goodies,
will force you to labor blindly to collect these; just to self-appease.
And you will be pulled in things around, auto-magically, like in a
black hole. Surely, you gain ownership, but inside, lives with a lost
and a cluttered soul.

Life becomes meaningful if hunger is realized before feeding the
food. As the response is relevant and reasonable for—what to exclude
or include.
In this simplicity, one realizes that life's real food court
is not far away, but available right now and here—just next door.

O Beloved, allow your spirit:
A final "salvation" from its never-dying incarnations, born out—of
archaic mythologies, and earthly inventions.
A final "salvation" from an image of a socially valued commodity,
and let it live imageless, as a free being, belongs to existential reality.

A final "salvation" from canonical formulae prophesied by books
and mystics, and let it live by the awareness of open life, rather
than by learning hidden tricks.
A final "salvation" from ownerships and exertion,
and let it act earnestly, without ensuing an actor, out of the action.

O Beloved cosmic whole, may all *beings* be blessed with a spirit:
One who is non-utilitarian, and non-local, seeking the perfume of
wisdom. And, matters of living and dying are non-matter for it, seeking
true freedom.
One who moves as a fresh and free wind across the jungles.
And, singing and dancing with trees, but never mingles.

Playing in the deep valleys and on the floating clouds, delivers the
pure breath to all, without favors or doubt.
Its only discipline is to remain free
and to allow itself to flower timelessly with thee.

The Divine Temple

The worshipper is worshipped here.

Prelude

The word "divinity" is most relevant to a religious mindset and is used in relationships with an external agency. Accordingly, we have created the expressions of it in the world and our hearts, in the forms of temples, pilgrimages, visions, angels, spirit guides, and so on.

It is commonly seen that we devote ourselves to these divine agencies unconditionally, and sometimes to extreme levels of blind followership. Thereupon, we create a division, in our minds, between it and the "rest of the existence." Generally, this division suggests a comparative contra- indication that the "rest of the existence" is inferior. We classify and categorize our perceptions, thoughts, and feelings through this division. Accordingly, our reactions follow it to make it a reality of life. How does this happen? It is due to a partitioning of the mind, which creates a divine switch that triggers divine feelings upon the invocation of a specific entity or a place. It is a classical associative conditioning of the mind. In this way, an externalized divine agency becomes your remote control, and in its presence, you behave differently. But, deep down, the turmoil may still exist in you, waiting for conditions to show and grow the real-old-self.

This point of view is superficial, conditional, partial, and of a psychological significance only. It does not transform the *being* intrinsically but temporarily fluctuates the feelings by associating with a chosen divine agency. For example, people go to the Himalayas to find peace, and some of them do find calmness in the foothills, but upon returning to the market, they are the same as before. Now, they want to go back again to loan the same experience of calmness, which is arduous. Interestingly, sometimes just by looking at the pictures, they feel calm. Then images of Himalayas can substitute the real one. In this way, Himalayas can be brought into our homes, and a daily ritual can trigger the calmness, conveniently. This type of divinity is a utility created in the house.

Any sane person will question this sort of divine propaganda. One would need a sincere, rational, and unbiased self-inquiry into the fundamental nature of *being* and its relationship to the existence, before devoting her/himself to any form of divinity. For this to happen, one need not establish any extraordinary goal, but must initiate with a very ordinary experience.

It is evident that knowingly or unknowingly, human beings remain continuously engaged in mundane experiences. Unfortunately, we simply consume the experience, one after another, without noticing its life cycle, and we build our story of life. Rarely we investigate the fundamentals of it and remain unclear about the knower and the knowledge.

So, why not initiate inquiry at a most basic level of experience—the world of objects, the body as a sensor, and mind as perceiver; and finally, what lies beneath the perceiver? Thereupon, r ealize i f t here is a nything special in the vast existence, called divine, or the existence itself is divine, including you? And, is "divinity" separate or external from a real *being*?

A question arises, why one needs to commit to this self-inquiry? Many organizations are teaching, preaching, and selling transcendental packages of divinity, why don't we use them?

Truthfully and practically, it is a personal endeavor and responsibility. It is a transformation of *being,* experientially—the unconditional nature of self and its relationship to existence. Firstly, remember your experience is not organizational but individual. If organizations had solved it for us, humanity would have evolved differently. For example, religious organizations have taken self-appointed responsibility for dusting this world out of ignorance and its resultant suffering, but it is obvious that religions themselves have become the source of much of this dust. Secondly, a thing must be found where it is lost. Therefore, the reality of *being* must be discovered within the framework of *being,* rather than going into organizations, caves, jungles, or monasteries, etc. The seeker, the goal, and the tools are within yourself. External things (including this book) can inspire and inform you, but the effort and real experiences are yours only.

This poem sketches a similar graph and the success story of the troubled mindset of a sincere seeker who sees that the existential reality and the way the world is evolving are misaligned. He cannot do anything about it due to his deep internal struggle in deciding to come out of his old habit and conforming mindset. He overcomes the roadblock to initiate the pathway on his own. And with a strong determination, he sets out to apply arduous effort to enquire about the nature of "self." Finally, he achieves success which allows him to live ordinarily, but in alignment to existence.

In this way, it delivers the message that you are the cosmic clay out of which everything is made—a devotee, the temple, divine element, and doer of all actions. The worshipper is worshipped in "You—living *being*" as a divine temple. It looks illogical and complicated, but true. Once the real *being* is realized as a source of divinity, then devotion is directed to oneself.

This poem serves as a similar message to one stated in *Ashtavakra Mahageeta,* chapter 8, verse 23.

"*Aho aham namo mahyam, vinasho yasya nasti me Brahmadistambaparyantam jagannasho'pi tishthataha*

I bow down to my Self. This Self in me is indestructible.

Even though this whole Universe may change, stones may change over time, but I am indestructible. There is nothing outside of me."

Readers should notice that here the word "divinity" is used very differently. Divinity is a unified development of a *being* who is aware, appreciates, and embraces existential totality. The words "unified" and "development" imply a practical and holistic development of *being* in all dimensions—physical, mental, and spiritual. And with a developed and refined pure consciousness, when the conscious *being* plugs the socket of spirit into existential reality, this can be called as "divine oneness." Human existence would be far more advanced if *beings* were nurtured to be existentially divine rather than encouraged to be dependent on made-up divine agencies.

Poem

It was a frigid and frosty night, and the world was fast asleep.
I was watching from my window, onto the mountain peaks.
The glittering stars looked upon the white mountains, covered with
fresh snow,
and the moon was flashing like a lamp, making the dark sky glow.
I had heard of many stories about the temple of the mountain, that
revealed the secrets to seekers, by raising the curtain.
But I never believed those stories,
I don't know why? Maybe it was my fear of the unknown or lack of
courage to try.
Yet, there was a fuzzy appeal to touch that mountain top,
though dull, this call was always in me, ticking like a clock.
And my hibernating soul used to slip the "ticking" behind,
as it got comfortable and captivated by the sluggish mind.
But, there was something that troubled my soul with a strange and
deep sinking pain,
and was dwelling for long, in the blind zones of my thinking lane.
Although, I admit that my intellect consoled my worry,
and like a soulmate always helped me to avoid it, and bury.
But, that night was very different,
my soul was intensely unquiet, and intellect lost the battle and
rather provoked my plight.
My clamoring soul craved for release and was dying to rest in
peace. Albeit, I was unsure of where to go, but was sure that
somewhere else, must I go.
As if my soul was locked inside and lost the key,
but who cares, when you intend to break the walls, to be free. This
unguarded suffering transformed into an uncaring hammer,
and broke the trust in my scholastic dictionary and its old
grammar. There was no purport left in living comfortable and

dormant down here, so, must I walk up in the hope of meaning
to appear?

This purposeless past, stirred the dormant volcano, in my inmost
vein, which pushed my body to start moving up the snowy
mountain.

For no salient reasons, I was in a hurry to reach the apex, and
witness the unknown,

perhaps that was the only way to react to my hollowness that was just
born. For the first time, the intellect gave up its pompous pretense to
rule, and agreed only to contribute as a servant, needful.

Soon, I traversed the realm of flora and fauna whether living or
dead, which appeared to be my borderline of attachment to the
social spread. Thereafter, I came to a vast void of snow, where the
chilly winds kept the emotions very low.

Yet deep down, my soul was fired up, which was the only fuel left
to fill my motivational cup.

Utterly lonely, I kept moving up on the soft snow leaving behind
my foot trail,

and the only companion walking with me was my shadow-tail.

After a long while, I reached the summit and looked around,
it was dead silence, which was challenged by my gasping sound.

But, I felt relieved that I had escaped the world of words and language,
and everything about that which kept me and my psyche engaged.

There was a humming sound in my spirit but no words in it.

This magical freedom from my self-image gave birth to a clear
heart of a seeker's sage.

This created a peculiar curiosity, to know the naked-pure self, in its
utter neutrality,

which is free of impressions and traits, and thus exists unmodified
in its aboriginality.

For the first time in my life, the soul, mind, and body poured pure
tears empty of any desire,

but with an existential curiosity burning as a silent fire.

Spoke in my heart, "O Beloved, show me the temple where I can worship thee in my solitude, and fulfill my journey to come this far, on this altitude." Suddenly, I felt fullness and a presence; lifted my head skyward beyond the earthly fence.

Chills of fear and surprise entered my eyes and fluttered in my gut as a rage of butterflies.

It was a colossal silvery temple that sat on the mountain top as a titanic castle. Its zenith touched the center of the milky moon and felt like floating from there like a celestial balloon.

And the white moonlight was dripping on to that shiny temple, standing on velvety snow, made it look like a bouquet of stars, descended upon me, for the cosmic glow.

I lifted my right foot towards that place, and suddenly a lump of snow splashed on my face.

And a command intuited in me, "Only the *being* who is able to be natural and naked could enter this temple."

Unhesitant, I left my clothes on the body and covers on my heart, outside, and stepped into the temple and walked to the altar inside.

I asked myself, who is the God of this temple to whom I must pray, and whom I surrender myself for the blessings to spray?

Oblivious to the rituals of that place, I bowed down with my closed eyes, and sang the humble psalms, most popular in the world of the wise.

Immediately another intuition struck me, "Thou must stop this folly, as no God exists to enslave you, nor your servility makes you holy.

This temple is a womb of alchemy where your direct realization will set you free. Which is by no one else, but your own exertion and clarity give birth to wisdom and vision of in-depth reality."

I lifted my face up and eased my jaw and was utterly astonished by what I saw.

Millions of magical mirrors whirling around like storm, and reflecting me at all levels in persisting and purging forms.

One set of mirrors reflected my physical body and its sockets of senses— vision, touch, smell, taste, and hearing; working as feelers on my fences. Thereupon mirrors reflected the body inside, which is like a city of systems working together, on which the spirit rides. The frame and form were made by countless cells, who were totally engrossed in Generation, Operation, Destruction and Renewal.

Having inherent and accrued intelligence, ready to give it to the next generation without any attachment or abhorrence. The exchange of matter was the law, and hoard it in any form was a flaw.

Only pure intelligence could let go so easily, where death is also embraced as a function of life, equally.

Then I saw another family of mirrors reflecting my emotions, filling up the juicy flavors and colors to my notions.

They were the spicy bubbles of energies, bursting into millions of moods and moments of mysteries.

Miraculous were these bioenergy knots, if they were wholesome, then they enhanced the hidden energy, and if unwholesome then they leaked the apparent energy, and if neither wholesome nor unwholesome, then they conserved energy. They could secretly move across waking, sleep, and dream states without *being* noticed by the volition gates, but if caught in our awareness, then they can show our unknown persona in its bareness.

Thereupon, I saw a set of mirrors reflecting my intellect which creates thoughts by associating and calculating concepts. Intellect is the supply chain of information, it uses the input to the process and gives output to help in making decisions. It gives reason to a choice and offers wit to our voice.

But, in the end, intellect is merely a computing engine, and it should only be used for its specific purpose and function.

And then I saw another set of mirrors reflecting the intelligence, in
the form of systems born out of physical and mental sense.
This intelligence is the regulatory guide,
and I realized, for the well-being, my systems must abide.
The disease occurs when I am misaligned to existential intelligence,
and work against my native essence.
Thus, I kept witnessing my existential forms intimately, again, and
again in the moving mirrors around me.
A wordless dialogue arose in me: "I am a collection of experiences
of my forms, but is there a central key?"
This self-reflection allowed for a vision to express that experience
exists in the forms, and the experiencer is formless.
Spoke to me, "Forms of experiences are composed, imposed, and
disposed, but experiencer is an imageless field in which these forms
are disclosed." The first time the true intelligence shone in me
without any image, and there was no movement in the space.
And without any movement, sense of time did not exist, therefore,
the experiencer was unbound by the space-time axis.
With this new pansophy, I stepped out of the temple with a new
awareness in me.
As I walked out in the snow with a new mind, I witnessed no more
footprints were left behind.
I realized, "my own weight creates impressions; else I live freely in
existence without any possessions."
I turned back, and the temple was gone, leaving behind a limitless
void, as if a vacuum had been created by a gigantic asteroid.
I kept watching the emptiness, and the last intuition came, that a
temple becomes truly divine, where the worshipper is worshipped
at the same time. O Beloved, let the individual be the divine temple
where worshipper is worshipped.

Section 2

Harmony in Becoming

I was that, but I became this.
I am this, but I wanted that.
Now, I wish; I become that.
- The story of my becoming

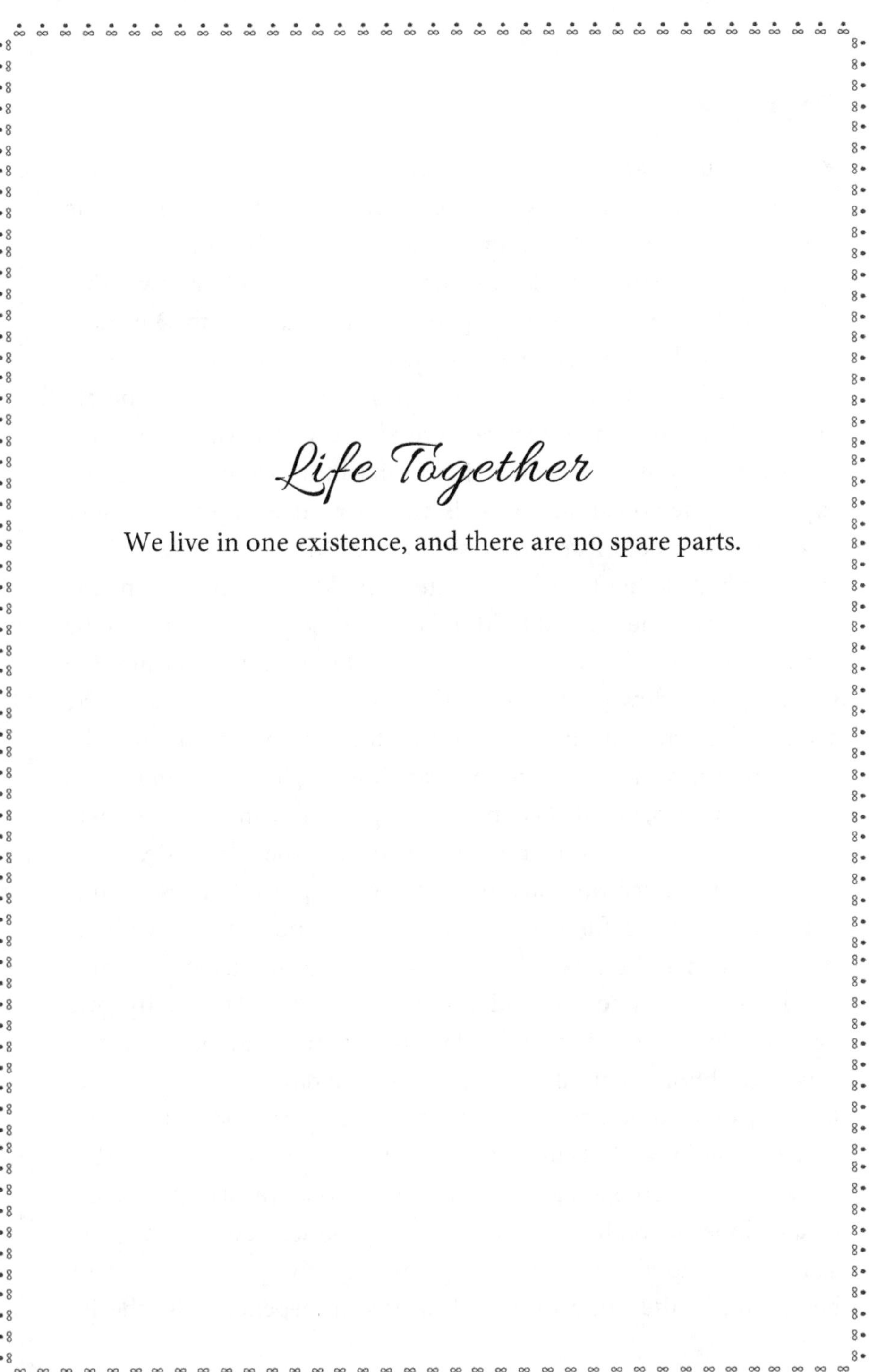

Life Together

We live in one existence, and there are no spare parts.

Prelude

Can you create a gap in existence? Can you possibly live unconnected in this world? Can colors be seen without the seer? Can you perceive anything without sensing the other?

Every breath we take links us with trees. Every drop of water we drink links us to the rivers. And, every step we move links us to earth. Our entire existence is in deep relation to one another, and isolation is impossible.

Even after tremendous technological advancement, it is nearly impossible to create a perfect vacuum at a very physical level; forget other dimensions of existence. Just think of an elementary school experiment demonstrated by kids with a regular straw. Sip water through it and hold it from the sipping end with your fingers. You may think that due to gravity, water should flow down from the open side, and then if you hold it from the open side, there will be a gap created inside the straw. But, it does not happen because the water will not flow down due to the pressure created, because the pressure becomes more powerful than the gravity, and it stops the water from flowing down until you are holding it. The moment you release your grip, gravity becomes more powerful, and the water will run out of the straw, and air will be filled from the other side.

Did you notice what just happened? The physical laws became alternatively powerful not to allow the vacuum to be created. It appears that there is a higher intelligence in existence, which regulates the role of secondary physical laws like gravity and pressure to favor the primary law of Oneness; in other words, existence abhors vacuum. This can be seen in day to day experiences in many other modifications of existence. Isn't it magical to realize that existence manifests into unique forms, as diverse as possible but still retains "interdependence" as a foundational reality? It does not create clones or replicas for its finished products; even twins grow as different individuals. As if uniqueness is its way to respect every being and at the same time makes us interdependent to cherish oneness. No *being* is created as a spare part in existence; all are its primary expressions.

On the contrary, we try hard for sameness and equality and still live divided. We have mechanical designs to create sameness in machines, utilities, languages, religions, trade, and treaties for commonality, but still, there is a tremendous rift between us. For example, in families, we speak the same language, eat the same food, and so on. But, a painful break-up still happens. Why?

We are also offspring of vast existence; still, we are incapable of living by this fundamental reality of Oneness, and somehow managing to live through gaps. Why is this sense of Oneness, not a natural way of our living? Where are we missing the link? What is the reason for this global power outage under which we fail to see our togetherness? There must be something we have done to ourselves, which has kicked the oneness in our blind spot.

Let's think upon it; how can we embrace the uniqueness and diversity of each one of us and still fundamentally live as One humanity? Shouldn't we reflect upon and explore the existential design?

Human beings have indeed changed the face of this planet more than any other species; we've proved to be most intelligent among all. Also, it is equally valid that human beings live with the fear of other human beings the most and have been the most devastating to each other; thus, we've proved to be the most stupid species among all. It appears, deep down in our social psychology, we have repeatedly rooted an idea of comparison, separation, and nurtured selfishness. Therefore, like a wise farmer who sprays fertilizer and uproots weeds in the same season, we need to enhance our intelligence and weed out the stupidity of selfishness in our lifespan.

Our best guide is this vast and *unified existence* itself. We need to learn its functioning of unity in diversity at a deeper level. Can we mimic existential design to create a culture of One humanity as a fundamental law, and other rules of nations, religions, economy, and so on takes secondary roles? Similar to the elementary school experiment explained earlier.

In this poem, a simple yet deep meaning of togetherness is elaborated, like the waves are born out of the ocean, and fall back in the ocean. They exist without separation. It is not a hypothesis but an all- pervading intelligence that can see the whole in parts. Existence works through balancing the forces based on togetherness only.

A *being* who values a part in the whole and realizes the function of the whole in part attains to supreme wisdom.

Poem

O Beloved Existence,
whisper this vital breath in all *being*s.
Songs become sweet

only when ears taste them.
Relations are fulfilled

only when Oneness embraces them.

Life goes on and on,

exists together and never alone.
You are not you, and I am not me.
I am in you, and you are in me.

You give something of you

when you greet someone.
And when someone greets you,
you allow them to enter.

Thus, greet all *being*s

to expand.
And gather greetings

to be grand.

Life happens through my awareness,

and I am aware through its happening.
Togetherness is a natural occurrence,

and isolation is an impossible thing.

In this vast soup of life

nobody is forbidden,
and beheld in unique equality,

could be exposed or be hidden.

Once we develop this realization,
we feel a deep interconnection.
Thereupon, at our best, we attain to
Oneness expressed as compassion.

There is no subtraction,
nor even addition,
only the play of existence
to balance out the equation.

The forces behind manifestation
follow a basic trend.
End meets the origin,
and origin becomes the end.

And those who ask, who am I?
If they know that I am you,
would let this "I" die away,
as this is the only real clue.

And knower of this truth,
in life, lives happily ever.
At death, dies fearless,
and beyond these, exists forever.

O, Beloved, the only awakening is to realize existential oneness,
the rest are all suboptimal attempts, still toward it.

To-Be...

There are no events in existence, only processes,
though we gauge our life pivoted around the events.
No *being* ever becomes anything, as it never escapes *becoming*.
Can you see in between the events into *becoming* of *being*?

Prelude

To quote Heraclitus, "No man ever steps in the same river twice, for it's not the same river, and he's not the same man." It means that the human being is in a state of *becoming* but has never become anything. It is a great insight but rarely realized.

This insight rhymes with our daily life, but mostly in a negative way. Everyone is struggling to become something or someone else, from childhood. It has become our core expertise to live under stress of *becoming* this or that. You can start your day by writing, "I want to become ," and you will see that this blank space will never be filled;

rather, your cup of desire to fill it will always be full. Also, this burden of *becoming* is very elastic—you can feel it for a moment, for a day, for a year, or for your entire life. This perspective of becoming is not only spurious but self-destructive.

No one can bypass *becoming*; its understanding is meaningful for everyone. Moreover, alignment to *becoming* is an art of living. Now look oppositely. Is there anything that can be called *non-becoming* that you are aware of? Can the living be possible out of *non-becoming*? Can you enforce *non-becoming*? If the answer is a big NO, then it is a must to understand *becoming* and learn to align with it, to create the best version of yourself.

Let's take a closer look at the practical wisdom of *becoming and* leave out academic arguments. What is *becoming*?

Simply, *becoming* means transformation of things from one to other forms, following a set of rules, and implies impermanence. It is a fundamental law in existence. Through it, existence is connected, and interdependence is possible. For example, you eat food, food is digested, and it becomes you. Your waste makes fertilizers, and plants consume fertilizers, which makes food for you again. The story of *becoming* continues at the physical level.

Similarly, you are angry with a friend. Your anger becomes a thought. Your thought becomes a speech in action, which becomes food for your friend's ears. Your friend becomes angry and reacts. Now, a bitter relationship becomes a reality. The story of mental *becoming* continues between you two.

Becoming is expressed in many ways. It can be physical or mental like facial makeup, expressions, outward actions, or the transformation of beliefs, values, and attitudes. Or, it can be fast or slow—competition or aging over time. Or, lastly, it can be natural or volition-based—aging, autonomic functions of the body or playing gamble to be rich. In all cases and categories, *becoming* can be understood as a rational phenomenon, not random. We may not grasp it due to our limited awareness of it. But not-knowing is not equal to non-existence or non-sensible. Therefore, we can assume that there is a law or order of *becoming* in existence; it can be understood by expanding our awareness. The benefit of understanding it is that the *being* can minimize the struggle and suffering in life by aligning with it. For example, when you walk downhill, you use the power of gravity to support your activity. Likewise, by knowing and aligning to the natural order of becoming, you leverage existential support in life.

It is eminent, but not easy to understand the law of *becoming*. It is like a keyring holding many valuable keys together. Let's unlock the doors of our awareness one by one by zooming into the features, functions, and values of each key.

The first key is *cause, conditions, and effect*. If a mango seed is sown inside the earth, with right supporting conditions, it will grow into a mango tree and will produce the mango fruit only, not a pomegranate. Likewise, the efficient cause of *wh at we are* is inside us, and we are supporting the conditions for the end result(s) we are getting in life. If you truly realize this key, then can you blame anyone for your anger or sadness? The answer is, "No." Instead, a deep sense of curiosity and responsibility to self-regulate will trigger in you. You will embrace the power of regulation at the physical, mental, and spiritual levels. And by changing your internal efficient cause and supporting conditions, you will make your life festive and happy.

The second key is *Relative Interdependence,* which means we are relatives and relatively depend upon each other for our social development. But ego and ownership-based societies have broken social interdependence into dependent and independent relations by using power equation in relationships. Can you live without being independent or dependent and with interdependence in everything you exchange in existence? The answer can be "Yes" only if you have a feeling of love and care instead of power play in your relationships. Also, this key is important to understand existential interdependence as well, but here it is used only for social interdependence — for example, our relationship to a tree or sun.

The third key is *the seer and seen relationship*; it is interesting to know that the attitude of the observer changes "what is observed" and vice-versa. Thus, every individual is responsible for *becoming* of the world into a good or bad place and vice-versa. How your life is *becoming* in the world is influenced by your attitude of the world. For example, a peaceful religious fanatic may have an allergic and angry reaction in a dance bar due to a negative attitude about the place. The world becomes beautiful or ugly, not due to the world which exists outside, but by the world which you carry inside you. And, you become beautiful or ugly, not due to your native existence, but due to the world you allow from outside, inside you.

The fourth key is *identity and transformation.* Is your identity intrinsic or loaned? Is it fixed or transformative? Is it singular or plural? How many layers of identity are you wearing? For example, when you say, "I am poor." Ask yourself, is it intrinsic to you or loaned poverty? Can you transform into a rich person? Is poverty the only identity you have, or you have other identities like father, national, religious, and so on? Are you poor by pocket or by belief?

Overall, one needs to enhance the awareness of the keys held together in the keyring of *becoming*. And, if a *being* is determined to become the best version of him/herself, then he/she can tune intention into existence and gain favors from this law. Thus, by regulating life with these keys, one can live joyfully.

This short poem indicates the nature of *becoming* and inspires everyone to live conscious of it. Thereupon, use this existential law to design society in a peaceful and conscious community where life is not lived as a socially mandated project to deliver, but as a joyful existential experience.

Note: This topic is so vast and deep that it deserves its own book of work. However, this poem delivers a taste of it, in a nutshell.

Poem

O Beloved,
if you scrape life to find reasons behind any dispute,
you would find that *becoming* is always its original root.
If there is anything that can be called as seminal sin,
you would find, *becoming* is the seed under its skin.

Becoming is an unavoidable centrifugal force,
which pushes out your attention, away from your core.
Usually, everything you wish to latch on is outside,
leaving your core unattended and unhappy inside.

Thus, without a song in your heart, you forget to sing,
but you learn to speak and shout as a mechanical thing.
Sadly, this is the same story for most of the *beings*,
no wonder the world is orbiting in crazy *becoming*.

Every soul who is humming
is a wave in this ocean of *becoming*.
And, until this *becoming* is natural and free,
the addiction of desires will push yourself, "to be..."

Ergo, in this world of desires, you are always pushed "to be...,"
And, to cope up, you deploy a borrowed self, and devalue your
original "me." Thus, yourself is polarized between a core and a
crust.
It creates psychological tension due to the opposite thrust.

The outer demands are powerful and more,
eventually, makes you forget your inner core,
though the suffering continues,
because the deep-down core is still in use.

O Beloved, let us make our world a place of healthy *becoming*,
which keeps our attention on crust and core as one thing.
Where we are not torn apart as subjects of suffering,
and our life becomes a means to attain its true meaning.

We have unique intelligence to make a choice,
so let us make our living as a festival to rejoice,
which happens only when joy is flowering from the core,
and our crust is nourishing it from all directions, even more.

You know the garden of joyful *becoming*
is right behind the door of pure *being*.
Knowing this effortless *being* inside
is like a great homecoming.

Thus, from this pure *being*
all *becoming* grows.
Rooted in this center
all the vitality flows.

Choose to become such a pure *being*,
becoming of that becomes a non-becoming.
Appears to be activated through effortless volition,
which grows naturally and not as a rugged reaction.

What is this pure *being*, "to be"?
Which is like nectar hidden in the sea?
What is this pure being, "to be"?
Which can be the glue for your glee?

So, what is "to be" of a pure *being* in the world of *becoming*?
O' Beloved, know it carefully.

To be "born" is to die totally to your past moments.
To be "dead" is to be born anew with no residual ends.
And to be a "living" is to know continuity beyond these two ends.

To be at "home" is to rest in peace.
To be at "peace" is to be one-piece.
And to be one-piece, the ego must cease.

To be for someone is to loosen up and dissolve.
To be of someone is to open up and involve.
And to be in love— is to love, and be loved, and be the love.

To be a parent is to be a keeper of a gift of existence.
To be a child is to be loving the "creator" in your parents.
And to be a family is to cherish concord in many fragments.

To be friends is to become a two-leaf door, and keep the unwanted, far away offshore.
To be neighbors is to be the first aid in pain and firsthand to dance on the festival's floors.
And to be social is to let go of your loneliness, and never let anyone feel ignored.

To be a workplace is to produce worth and value.
To be a war is to be a prop of righteousness and virtue.
And to be welfare, you give a hand to others without your hands having a clue.

To be a government is to apportion the richness of riches and poverty of the poor.
To be commercial is to create convenience and confer the security to secure. And to be religious is to cherish spirit, and make life more meaningful and mature.

To be a teacher is to empty generously and live as a disciple.
To be a disciple is to reflect the teacher as an example.
And to be a school is to provide life skills to make you able.

To be a seeker is to burn in seeking.
To be a seer is to focus the spirit in seeing.
And to be a sage is to be a fruit ready for "giving."

To be a devotee is to surrender for completeness. To be a yogi is to shed the self for love of oneness. And to be a Bodhi is to live as a lamp of awareness.

O Beloved, may all realize the discipline of pure *being*, and enjoy the worldly *becoming* a joyful living.

Four Selves: Ill, Indulgent, Illuminated, and Immersed

When I close my eyes, I converge.
When I open my eyes, I diverge.
When I see with closed eyes, I emerge,
When I am the eyes, I submerge.
Peculiar is the play of *becoming*.
Isn't it?

Prelude

While driving on the roads of Delhi in India, you will notice big electric advertisement boxes on the sideways, hanging outside the shops. These are kind of suitcase-shaped aluminum boxes, with only the front side made up of a soft-white glass-sheet with colorful alphabets designed on them, depicting the messages. And, inside the box will be a big white tubelight beaming strong light on the glass panel. These boxes flashes messages in various colors and designs outwardly, but if you look inside the big box, you will just notice the glow of pure white light. This simple apparatus makes us think, why on the outside there is so much color variation, but inside is oneness of light? The answer lies in the traits—shapes, colors, and impressions of images and alphabets through which the light is passing. These various colorful lights also mix with each other to create more variety outside.

We, human beings, are also the same as these electric boxes. We have pure consciousness like the white light glowing inside, but when it is passed through the individual traits, it radiates the modified individuality. So, in a way, we all are individual consciousness when seen through our traits, but in another way, we all are one consciousness when seen from behind the traits. It also concludes that there is no separation between individual self vs. cosmic self; the observer creates the differences based on his or her reference point to observe the consciousness. This also explains our perception of consciousness in terms of duality—bonded by traits, and non-duality—beyond traits.

This poem primarily focuses on the traits that classify human consciousness into four broad categories of the self: *ill, indulgent, illuminated, and immersed,* covering the entire spectrum of dual and non-dual traits of being and its becoming. These selves can also be perceived as individual consciousness of beings when seen from a worldly perspective, as the images and messages of an electric advertisement box, when seen from outside, as mentioned above.

An *ill* consciousness can be symbolized with an inert rock—full of resistance and non-participation in life. It opposes the growth mindset by denying anything new in life. It can waste the entire life-term in a static mode of living.

An *indulgent* consciousness can be symbolized with an animal—acts and reacts for sensual demands only. Its prime motives are greed and selfishness. Therefore, its focus of life lies outside in the world, constantly consumed in desires and enjoyments of material possessions. An *illuminated* consciousness can be symbolized with a ripened human intelligence—it seeks the spirit inside and makes the inner aliveness as the center of life. It takes human life as a bridge to rise to higher states of consciousness, and matters of the world are a means for self-fulfillment. Thus, it balances its inner and outer world through a discipline. Regulation and realization are its chief virtues.

An *immersed* consciousness is the ground consciousness of the other three, which can be called existential intelligence. It is a continuum, surpassing the division of the inner or outer world. It is oneness behind the "thingness" of the other three individualized consciousness.

These four selves are not permanent operating centers, rather dynamically interactive traits in human beings. Every activity—perception, thinking, feeling, and sensing, is influenced by a predominant self-hood.

For example, sometimes, we feel dull, depressed, or heavy like a rock; or we feel violent and aggressive to snatch things from others like animals; or we feel introspective, kind, or compassionate for others; or we get immersed in existential nature during dreamless sleep. But, continuous conditioning of one type makes it the default mode of expression of our individual consciousness.

Now, if we look at the world from the lens of the definitions of these four selves, we will find that largely the collective human consciousness is stuck as *indulgent* and secondly *ill*. On the other hand, we will find that rarely someone cares to live as an *illuminated* or *immersed* self.

This crookedness in collective human consciousness clearly indicates that the worth of human existence is limited and pivoted around made-up material goals to serve the traits of indulgence. In this type of culture, one is bound to live a life infected by jealousy, insecurity, social neurosis, and financial issues, resulting in endless suffering.

It is time to resolve this crookedness of human consciousness by valuing and becoming illuminated and immersed selves. This will upgrade the human existence to be radiant existentially than *becoming* artificially.

This poem elaborates on the nature of *becoming* into these four forms of selves. And, there are twenty applications given at the end of the chapter for their in-depth understanding.

It's a long poem, read it very slow and patiently.

Poem

O Beloved transient *beings*,
in this river of life, we all change within a wink,

manifesting as bitsy bubbles of impressions and energy.
And a simple law of arising and dying maintains this synergy.

This endless river flows from emptiness, for eons,
whose beginning, becoming, and the ending is unknown.

Betwixt the ends of coming and going,
we forge our particularity by becoming and doing.

This becoming provokes a sense of self and separation,
thus, coils our thinking and feeling around an egoistic sensation.

Rare are the beings who could see it dwelling inside
as an illusory effect.
And common are the beings who cuddle their ego
and the sensation of this defect.

This self creates a weird reality of our impressions,
which further distorts the directness of our experiences
and expressions.

Hundred are the names, but four are the states,
and your entire life is just a play of their traits.

But, the quality of traits in your "self" varies in these four states,
somewhere it is solid as a rock, and elsewhere
it may carry no weight.

Poem

These four states are: ill, indulge, illuminate, and immerse.
They are the essence of your experience, extracted from the universe.

Human suffering is a side effect of their deceptions.
Thus, it's a virtue to explore them in your "self" and its modifications.

On Modification of an Ill Self

In the first class of "self," there lives a life, being lazy and sick,
she stays aloof to the inner and outer world, just like an idle brick.

She makes life so heavy that it gets sucked in a shell and suffocates.
Thereby, she lives secluded, on the side, by shutting off all gates.

Nothing else can kill her, but self-imprisonment.
Because, instead of swimming out in the river of life, she chooses
to drown in a personal tank.

She lives ignorant and believes in delusions of the world, "out or
in," and the inner tendency is not to respond, which reduces her
life into a trash bin.

Involves in self-eccentricity, and lacks trust in her own
sisters and brothers,
but she brashly evolves as a parasite for living and depends on others.

Her inert life pumps meaningless breaths,
outwardly, she may appear peaceful, but inwardly she
feels fear of death.
An easy prey of diseases and addictions,
and with an uncaring attitude, she recklessly falls for
cheap seductions.

Life of self-denial is at the root,
and living a hellish life is the fruit.

A mindless being easily permits her,
and lethargic being helps to admit her.

The prevailing norms of her life are:
sleep over waking and defeat over caring,
and lonely over loving, and cowardly over daring.

She accepts dead winter over the spring,
and easily agrees to give up, even before her life zings.

O Beloved *ill-being*,
much longer are the days and nights when you sleep idly in your
cave, but it won't be long enough before the messengers of death
would unlock the seal of your grave.

"Now" is the time to shock your "self,"
and surpass illness to attain your health.

Fill enthusiasm in your drives,
and announce "Yes" to this life before death arrives.

On Modification of an Indulgent Self

The second "self" lives as an indulgent spree.
And, it dwells abnormally as an inverted tree.

With her roots hanging out in the world,
and her growing crown inwardly curled,

She has the psyche of a sating sponge, with a porous skin.
she inhales the desires with mouth wide open, outside in.

These random desires motivate her to move,
following her blind passions in the preset grooves.

She sucks the outer world to fill her greedy spirit inside,
thus, she is easily lured by popular passions for the sake of pride.

Through the five sockets of senses, she always opens out,
repels the true center of her "self" and hankers roundabout.

For her, the triggers of happiness are externally seated,
thus, she believes in competition and likes to be segmented.

Indulgence in its lesser form brings enthusiasm to fulfill the needs,
but if unregulated, it becomes an obsession to fulfill
the bottomless greed.

Indulgence in its highest form is like scabies of the soul,
which makes one scratch the rashes, for the irritation to control.

Though the restless soul bleeds and pules in pain,
she wanders to accumulate much but stays without gain.

Endless sensations manifest in her like a disease,
and she becomes the prey to ingrained habits to appease.

In a true sense, she does not want anything from outside,
but she wants to ease the pain of greedy sensations burning inside.
Thus, as a helpless servant,
she is bound to serve the life of the indulgent.

All her efforts in life are to run around luxury and utility,
and beyond it, she sees nothing; she ignores self-exploration as
futility.
Her ignorance promotes indulgence,
though it is fake, she still gets accepted because of convenience.

Hence, she fails to see the reality of living in this vast existence,
and she superficially passes over life, blinded by obsession.

Her lust for indulgence could last for a lifetime;
it remains the same, either fight for diamonds or
over nickel and dime.

Indulgence expresses itself either as attachment or aversion,
and sometimes wears hypocritical masks to hide its real version.

The rules of the grammar of her life story are:
Splitting over meeting,
and jealousy over greeting.

Gluttony over giving,
and retention over relieving.

Competition over unity,
and deceit over honesty.

Passion over purity,
brutish mind over maturity.

O Beloved indulgent *being*,
What remains in dry wood, if thrown into the fire?
Likewise, what remains in your life, when burnt in desires?

No one should indeed die in pain and poverty,
but equally true, that piling up is also not the prime priority.

The energy is indeed eternal but not in "you" for eternity.
Before it leaves you, let go of your indulgence for inner purity.

Stop worrying and running for a mindless chase.
Open the doors of senses to let the awareness flow in both ways.

And, know the magic of contentment and discipline,
to invest wisely in self-assessment, and look within.

The treasure of life is within you,
drop indulgence to be available, and turn inward to view.

O Indulgent *being*,
It is futile to be caught between illumination and indulgence.
And it is uneasy to keep swinging between this or that
or live on the fence.

You should be very cautious and beware of illumination,
because once tasted, there is no respite until its full resolution.

Thus, may you be determined and be illuminated.
May you rise and shine on this path until liberated.

On the modification of an Illuminated Self

The third "self" is a dancing flame,
and expansion of awareness is her leading aim.

She fires an authentic and real revolution inside,
allows the being to evolve out from all possible sides.

She takes this life as an opportunity,
to experience existence as a harmonious unity.

In her presence, the being becomes aware, and lives awake,
and conceives the awareness, to sieve the real from the fake.

Thus, cultivates the awareness of "self," different from personality,
which allows the being to see the individual "self" versus
the "self" in totality.

Moreover, the unconditional "self" is unveiled in her illumination.
Thus, life attains meaningfulness with the right discrimination.

This insight becomes a trusted friend, philosopher, and a guide, but
it is also a slippery surface for being's personas to slide.

She arranges the meaning of life around the lucid soul,
and awards the value to other things in life, a peripheral role.

Thus, a deep sense of contentment and balance prevails,
because of the attitude that my mirth or misery is
caused by other's fails.

She spreads the glow, but itself never inflates,
endures in free forms and moves lightweight.
Like a giant tree, she rises up and above, but deeply rooted in the
earth, her wisdom is compassion personified, and innocence is the
same as it was at her birth.

Her flame is pure and refined,
burns down anything unwanted and even leaves their ashes behind.

She enables the being to see the flow and source of consciousness,
and empowers to blow out the clutter of useless and
the clutch of craziness.

Intentions move frictionless without any fraction,
being's efforts are aligned between mind, speech, and action.

Feelings of bliss become the primary mode of expression;
attachment and aversions fail to create deep impressions.

She makes the essence of life practically visible,
rooted in consciousness—continuous and indivisible.

Its highest form perceives all beings as part of one non-being,
and the non-being an expansion of one being.

The being functions as if humanity is a big hive
where she is a worker bee, going deep inside to settle on the flower
of the soul and suck sincerely.

Thereupon, for a higher purpose, give it generously to make
the honey, and tirelessly fill the hive for the community
to live in harmony.

The traits of the illuminated "self" are:
To live in the natural order of existence, and embraces
higher integration, although immensely moral,
she lives non-obedient to any fake imposition.

To love the company of the wise and qualified,
and to avoid the gossips and futile talks of pride.

Even though this "self" knows the alpha and omega of cosmic
design, in the company of indulgence, she remains
mute and wishes to resign.

On the modification of an Immersed Self

The fourth self is immersed in the cosmic consciousness
like how a salt crystal, thrown in the ocean, loses its thingness.

Thus, she dissolves into the measureless,
and lives as the background for the other three to express.

She has no center of her own and hence no periphery.
She lives through others, but herself remains untouched and free.

She becomes one with the source of qualities,
but remains free of their particularities.

She is the thinker in thinking and the feeler in feeling,
and the sensors in sensing, and the perceiver in perceiving.

She does not seek or defy any experience,
but lives through all experiences.

She is felt as the construed image out of the other three,
and is the ground of their imagery, yet unconditional and free.
She lives choiceless and easy,
though liberated, her lifestyle is sophisticated simplicity.
She lives effortless and ordinary,
albeit unknown to the foreground. It is, indeed, the primary.

She is the soil. She gives herself to the fruits and weeds equally, and
lives unrecognized and underneath, giving to all impartially.

She is available as a colorless foundation
and assumes the name of the quality by its relation.

For example, she is love while loving,
and hate while hating,
and laughter when happiness abounds,
and tears when sadness surrounds.

She is like a mirror with no ownership of the image
but attains the form of whosoever comes to gaze.

When alone, she does not feel lonely,
although she remains alone in the crowd or company.

She is nobody's friend but is always friendly.
She doesn't favor anyone but is never an enemy.

She doesn't go anywhere, but she never stops.
Successes don't puff her up, and upon failures, she never drops.

She is the sky for the smiling rainbow,
and the sun, which makes the day to glow.

She is the year for the seasons to swing.
She is the warm love condensed in a wedding ring.

Truly, this self is a non-self as she is neither the knower nor the
known, but rather, she lives as a process of knowing the two together.
She remains alone.

O, Beloved, this self is the epitome of humanity, and most refined
forms expressed as unity in diversity.

On applications of the Four Selves

1. On goal-based life:
Illness runs away from responsibility, thus lives allergic to goals.
Indulgence craves for the material world, thus lives crazy with
countless goals. Illumination moves mindfully toward
the "why" and "who" of the object and the source.
Immersion has no aims of its own.

2. On the center of living:
Illness settles to live as a dependent, with the center of life outside.
Indulgence desires to live independently,
with the center of life outside.
Illumination values interdependence, with the center
of life inside as its source.
Immersion lives without a center.

3. On activity:
Illness lives an inactive and lazy life.
Indulgence lives an outwardly active life.
Illumination lives an inwardly active life.
Immersion is the passivity to support activities of the other three.

4. On age and life:

Illness has a longer life than its age.

Indulgence has a shorter life than its age.

Illumination lives eternally.

Immersion is the timeless axis.

5. If life is compared to a tree:

Illness is the disease of leaves.

Indulgence is the thorn.

Illumination is the fruit.

Immersion is the root.

6. On social values:

Illness escapes from the company of others.

Indulgence likes winning others and wishes for
others to be the opposite of itself.

Illumination likes *being* with others and wishes
others would be like itself.

Immersion has no other and lives in all.

7. On life mathematics:

Illness accepts subtraction and *being* the lowest denominator.

Indulgence craves its ego multiplier and seeks division outside.

Illumination realizes higher operations of integration and equality.

Immersion is the applied mathematics of life.

8. On self-perception:

Illness lives in delusion.

Indulgence lives in illusion.

Illumination lives with self-awareness.

Immersion is the ground where the awareness cultivates.

9. On the state of *being*:
Illness is in a sluggish sleep.
Indulgence is in a dream; it sees everybody else, but itself.
Illumination is awake.
Immersion witnesses all *being*s.

10. On togetherness:
Illness is OK with living as a blind spot.
Indulgence fears loneliness and *being* ostracized.
Illumination is contented, if alone, else loves
the company of the wise.
Immersion is the glue.

11. On challenges:
Illness accepts the defeat.
Indulgence celebrates the victory, and anything else causes worry.
Illumination is festive in the game of life and enjoys
outcomes as experiences.
Immersion is the game, and outcomes are its living modes.

12. On the balance of life:
Illness accepts imbalance and adversity.
Indulgence loves imbalance as a means in its favor.
Illumination maintains the balance of tides.
Immersion is composed of balance and the two sides.

13. On self-concept:
Illness lives in self-denial.
Indulgence is comparative and denies others for itself.
Illumination glows with a dignified self.
Immersion is empty of self-concept.

14. On self-confidence:

Illness lives in constant fear.

Indulgence is brave enough to face challenges.

Illumination is fearless about life situations.

Immersion lives outside of the circumstances.

15. On the garden of life:

Illness is a weed meant to be uprooted.

Indulgence is a thorn to be cautious of.

Illumination is the fruit and flower to be nurtured.

Immersion is the fertile ground.

16. On the effect of time:

Illness lives life as if it is already the past,

dead, and impossible to change.

Indulgence lives life, as if in the future, active and ready to change.

Illumination lives life in the now and acts in the present, ultimately.

Immersed is beyond the time scale.

17. On religious self:

Ill has no religion of its own.

Indulgent uses religion to fulfill its desire and indulgence.

Illuminated tends to live by the truth and trust of religion.

Immersed is the novelty of the religion.

18. On national self:

Illness does not belong to any nation.

Indulgence designs borders to divide the world into nations.

Illumination designs seam to unite the nations into the world.

Immersion is one border-less world.

19. On economic self:
Illness looks upon others and lives on leftovers.
Indulgence prefers polarization, and consumption over
production. Illumination adores distribution, exchange,
and gains by giving.
Immersion is the economic circulation.

20. On emotional self:
Illness lives in depression, disgust, and dismay.
Indulgence lives in passions, pain, and pleasures.
Illumination lives blissfully in gratitude and compassion.
Immersion lives as a base current for others to flow.

My Turban of Knowledge

Learning gave me the pride of knowledge.
Knowing made me humble, as I know now, how much I don't
know.

Prelude

According to Lao Tzu, "To attain knowledge, add things every day. To attain wisdom, remove things every day."

Our understanding of life is expressed through knowledge and wisdom. Both of these are important in their respective uses, but great confusion and suffering can arise if we misuse one for the other. Particularly on the path of self-inquiry, these two modes of understanding should be clearly and distinctly understood.

Knowledge is understanding a thing on the basis of collected information using our intellectual power. It can be owned, stored, analyzed, computed, and transferred. Therefore, it can have economic value and provide us with choices. Today, the access to knowledge is accelerating at explosive speed. People are walking with encyclopedias in their pockets. Credit goes to the smart gadgets floating in the market. Knowledge has clearly proved its supremacy in the world to the extent that the entire world is living in a fog of ideas, and has reduced human beings into thought bots. We relate to each other with ideas, languages, and descriptions. When you see a rose, you don't see a rose as such, but see it as a valentine's gift or a decorative item, etc.

On the other hand, wisdom understands the thingness of a thing, directly using our beingness in entirety—physical, mental, and spiritual. Hence it enables *real- ization*—which brings awareness of reality at this very moment free from past conditioning. When you see a rose, you do see the rose as such as a flower in existence. At a mature level of awareness, wisdom is in a meaningful realization of—*being*, existence, and their inter-relationship. It needs a deeper engagement in the phenomenon. The trajectory of wisdom is trusting our common sense, exploring, deep reasoning, experiencing the uncommon sense, formulate the meaning, thereupon expressing as a transformed *being*.

Both knowledge and wisdom have their specific functions, applications, and benefits for the development of human beings.

At a very high level, if we take existence as a mix of—matter and consciousness. Then, the effort in exploration of these two aspects can be very different, either knowledge-driven or wisdom-driven or both. And, circumstantially the effort could be deployed, How?

To explore the matter, knowledge can be beneficial. For example, if someone says consumption of cyanide causes death, then you need not actually consume it to realize it. You can be knowledge-driven, no need to re-invent the wheel. Leveraging Prior knowledge helps to focus your efforts by eliminating the non-useful means.

On the other hand, to explore consciousness, wisdom is of prime significance. Knowledge may be a by-product of knowing and realizing. Many times, a knowledge-driven effort is a hindrance in self-awareness because the intention is not to learn "about the awareness" but to realize "the awareness." For example, when you meet your loved ones. You feel the connection, and it occurs in the present moment, fresh and fulfilling. On the other hand, if you meet with a preconditioned mind and expectations, the experience may not be fresh and fulfilling. To some people the entire world looks boring due to a pre-concieved idea of it.

Sadly, we intermix our attitudes about exploration, which causes a lot of issues for humanity. For example, religions preach about spirituality and inward-looking approach. And the first thing they do is to give books, beliefs, stories, sermons, and scriptures; thus, it conditions the mind in a specific direction, aligned to their group thought. In this way, knowledge is used as a tool, and the power of suggestions is used to draw a particular experience out of *being*. People spend their entire life in accumulating theories but are never self-aware. It can be to the extent that common sense is transformed into common non-sense and people end up doing those things due to beliefs which they would not have done otherwise as individuals. Religious violence is a perfect example where a common person can be conditioned to become a religious weapon. Knowledge creates a biased attitude and hinders freedom of self-exploration. Its continuous injections solidify the biases and limit the mind to act and live free in the present moment. Our unlimited human potential gets locked out in the tight jacket of knowledge-driven society, which makes us feel claustrophobic and stressed out.

No wonder, most of the people on a self-realization path suffer from prevalent knowledge, and when they look out for help, unfortunately, they are given suggestions from the same bag of knowledge, which causes adverse conditions for them. For example, in religions, more rituals are provided as a remedy , at least initially. to fix other religious issues. Rarely, one realizes it as insanity and hindrance. And, until one throws away this knowledge-driven attitude in totality and resets to a wisdom- driven perspective, anything of real meaning is not gained.

This poem addresses this specific issue. It elaborates that since time immemorial, humanity has been evolving through religions, economics, nations, society, and so on. Therefore, a heap of knowledge is available to us, which can be attractive, or sometimes imposed from outside.   It becomes a mandatory dependency and a burden at the same time, but one needs to know that knowledge can be a prop but not a dependency; and mostly, it becomes a hindrance. On the path of self-awareness, the ONLY dependency is one's real intention, genuine effort, and availability to self-explore. Therefore, one needs to come out of the academic and defined mindset, accept the way he or she is without manipulation. This allows one to live original, fresh, and lively.

In short, live with a wisdom-driven practical life, born out of "knowing" instead of knowledge. Perhaps through us, the existence wants to experience the matter, so why not create original and joyful experiences in existence? You are the best creation of existence, and you can be the best creator of experience. How wonderful it is!

Poem

I was walking naked, barefoot, and empty-handed, but with a small turban of knowledge on my head. I diligently followed the road of evolution under the bright sun and a clear sky.

Through my course of this evolutionary trail, I engineered religions, nations, commerce, and societies; and tirelessly labored for their adulthood.

Every step forward was a moment of pride and celebration. My head shined as molten gold with vanity, and my heart was amused and sang the glory of weight upon my head, out loud.

Along with the maturity of knowledge, my turban was growing heavy, husky, and large. But, the body below my head remained unchanged.

With a desire to keep my head up, rare were the occasions when I looked down at my body and its native intelligence.

Gradually the molten gold seeped inside my heart, and clutched my blood vessels, and crippled the songs of happiness and celebrations of my life.

My heart pumped suffering all over my body, and my bare feet shivered and weakened, as they bled.

My legs forgot the freshness and festivity of life. Thereupon, fear and stress of ponderous weight prevailed. My body became a running factory of pain and sorrow.

I looked upon my titanic turban for a remedy, who pacified me by accusing laws of the world, and diagnosed that I was a mere puppet in the hands of my destiny. Thereupon, I was given medicine to adjust to the pain.

Great was my trust in my turban of knowledge, and my unquestionable respect convinced me that this pain was inherent in my body, and I was a natural sufferer on the path of life.

I could not think any other way but accepted whatever came from a trustworthy authority.

This friendly turban, with its hundreds of folds of religions, nations, commerce, and societies, gave me a new meaning and means to my life.

It favored my weak legs by giving me strong and long crutches of gurus, guides, and coaches as avatars of humanity.

And they showed enough care and sympathy for my bleeding soul and promised me a nicely groomed life, with a condition to follow them unquestionably.

Religion with a soft but cunning voice even promised me liberation from the rotten body shivering in pain at the "end" of the road.

These crutches decompressed me, and consoled my choked breaths, flowing through my heart, but numbed me to the slavery to which I was bound.

With this adoption, I, on the road of evolution, was living with manageable pain and plenary bondage of world systems, and their masters.

My turban got heavier and heavier, but now I had crutches to walk further, and evolve. My speed was slow but less painful, and eventually, I forgot that I had legs. I was used to these systems and their architects, as part of my natural daily life.

Old religions, tribes, trade, and social systems changed into new, but the suffering, slavery, and testimony of hope remained. And, to engage my interest and excitement, this turban of knowledge took new shapes and forms but from the same old garment, and kept its ownership.

With the comfort of crutches, my whole body forgot that I had legs as if they were paralyzed and unconnected from me. I never touched them to real ground.

Although in the back of my mind, I remembered the old pain, a sense of security due to this new support, and hope for liberation. This kept me moving further along.

Despite a fractal face, divisions, deceptions, and poverty all over, I never had to complain about the divisions and the misery of this turban on my head, because I learned to adjust to these systems and their architects, for the sake of convenience.

I forgot that I am born to this earth and not to a nation—and that I am from the shoreless ocean of consciousness, and not from gods of worldly religions—and that I am the human species born out of real intelligence of creation, and not of any social race—and my economy is barter betwixt need and its fulfillment, and not a commercial schema.

This deep ignorance corroded my soul, and my heart wept songs of unbearable suffocation and suffering with more tears than ever.

For the first time, and with great determination, I set out to find the cause of human sufferings amid all mental grief and misery. And, for the first time, I wanted to know my bondages more than liberation and put my real foot on the real ground.

Immediately my so-called paralyzed legs became red with blood. Within the same moment, a realization came to me that I couldn't stand the heavyweight of my turban. In the next second, I realized my own adopted weight would cause me to cripple. I, and no one else, am the carrier of my bondages—the turban of my knowledge.

I shook my head with all my energy and deepest intention and will and prayers, and all that I could gather to throw my turban on the ground, and I ended the long relationship.

Without delay, I became lightweight and could stand and walk and dance and sing on the same road effortlessly under the sun, with nature as it is.

Now, I remember my original state, and to my surprise, whatever was created even before my birth is still fresh, rich, unique, and undivided. In spite of all catastrophes, it is still novel and natural.

This freedom and movement came with the great wisdom that any order, mechanically invented by the intellect, is meaningless for existential reality. And anything meaningful is in order already within the cosmos here, now, and as always.

I looked upon the sky and touched the planets and stars and heard orderly resonating music. I looked down and kissed the tender blades of grass, breathing fresh air, and singing songs of freedom.

I looked at myself as a human being that is unique in space and time, living through existential order and felt shameful for not trusting it before. I realized that trust in oneself is the key to relate to existence.

Now I enjoy the freedom and friendship of this nature in its most real sense, but freedom is meaningless without wisdom, though I am wary of wearing any turban again.

I know, now, as a fact that true evolution can come out of the womb of liberation, which comes out of deep love for a radical revolution of self, in its natural order and virtue.

O Beloved, May *beings* cherish inherent intelligence and attain freedom from the imposed knowledge of world colleges made out of religions, society, commerce, and nations.

Bodhi and the Pilgrim's Caves

What is your religious philosophy?
Curiosity, seeking, exploration, and being a seer.
Or, a marketable need, followership, navigation,
and being a preacher.

Prelude

We all have an intrinsic curiosity to know about our roots, and its relation to the vast existential reality in which we are born, we live, and we die. This curiosity transforms a *being* into a seeker—one who intends to seek the truth. Many great seeker souls worked hard to explore their curiosity and attained meaning and realization. In this way, a seeker became a seer—one who sees the truth as it is. The seers translated their experiences into languages understood by others, which helped other seekers in their own search for meaning, and provided motivation.

On the other hand, many more *beings* with a mindset of a market projected this intrinsic curiosity as a well-defined "need," and organized paths in the form of organizations, cults, groups, and religions to fulfill it. In doing so, well-established maps were formulated by the respective organizations with a defined end-result. With a specific and known end-result provided by organizations, the *seeker* and *seer* framework got twisted into new forms. The forms were further reformed into various forms by the cunning blades of social blenders.

Curiosity became a marketable need, a seeker became a follower, and exploration became navigation. Human beings are more or less conditioned with this change now. But in this change, the *seer* is missed out as one who sees the truth as it is. Instead, a new role as preacher is born, one who speaks as learned. This model is more prevalent in today's society. Also, this type of becoming or change opened opportunities for scholars, pundits, and orators who themselves may not be either seekers or seers but became the best preachers of the navigation tools. They are accepted as a proxy for seers by the followers.

Of course, this modern operating model brought a significant change to *being*'s exploration efforts. Earlier the curious seeker used to explore the truth and became a seer. The direct realization was of prime importance. Now, organizations arrange the propaganda to create a need in the market and make followers who navigate through organizational paths to becoming *what* is unclear.

For example, Gautama, the Buddha, was intrinsically curious to know the root cause of human suffering. He became a seeker and worked hard to explore human suffering and became a seer and saw the root cause of suffering experientially, and its truth as i t is known. Thereupon, he came up with four noble truths about life and suffering and helped humanity. Whereas, in the second case, a *being* becomes a follower of established paths, enacts the truth as it is told to experience a predefined and suggested end result. The power of suggestion and its obedience is valued more than the exploration.

Therefore, in today's age, we must examine our efforts of self-reflection through the lenses of the two models. The true yardstick is our own attitude, guiding your efforts for it.

In the *seeker-seer* model, the seeker has a high degree of curiosity, sensitivity, receptivity, and self-discipline. He/she seeks clarity based on first-hand experiences than intellectualization; in fact, theoretical manipulation is avoided. Thus, lives adventurous, reasonable, and truthful to oneself. And, because the seeker is himself or herself responsible for practicing the right discipline, it is easier to eliminate the meaningless and unnecessary complications at a personal level and live a simple, yet profound life. The simplicity allows the seeker to focus energy to expand his or her awareness during an experience in the present moment. Thus, a wisdom-driven approach is embraced. Finally, a seer is discovered.

On the contrary, in a *follower-navigation path* model, the follower strives to achieve the given end-state goals; therefore, learning and working by the given methods to become fit to fill the defined gaps is desirable. The assumption is that if it is working for others, it should work for me. Follower's faith and acceptability are valued more than his or her individuality and reasoning. Rejection of unnecessary norms and rituals is difficult for individual followers because it is not in their discretion. Moreover, freedom is regulated.

However, a known and organized path gives more security and a social company that could provide for other social needs as well, and this makes it convenient and beneficial. But this social aspect of followership can lead followers into confused or conflicting situations. For example, in liberal societies, with so many competing and compelling paths, a follower can be confused about which one to choose, whereas, in conservative societies, paths can conflict with each other leading to hatred. Religious intolerance is not a hidden secret. Sooner or later, social power takes a central position because organizations grow through *followers* and become power centers to influence and engage with other factors like national, economic, and political interests. Eventually, they may lose their original purpose for establishment. The knowledge-driven approach is embraced. Knowledge becomes a sort of a commodity of organized factories. Finally, a *follower* is tailored.

Any sane and sincere person who has *curiosity* would wonder about these operating models. In this short story, three scenarios of the *follower-navigation path* relationships are examined. Firstly, *the follower of one path*—who blindly follows one path, and denies the remainder of existence, which makes him a nonparticipating, uncreative, and unnatural but faithful caretaker of the one path. Secondly, *the follower of many paths*—who samples many paths all his life, and gains the knowledge to become an outward scholar, while he lives inwardly confused, but creates a solid market, out of his preaching. And, thirdly, *many followers with many paths*—a hodgepodge society of many followers on several paths struggling with conflicting ideas, and need social discipline to reconcile intolerance of one another.

Poem

It was the time when sweet spring bloomed in her youth, and the warmth of sunshine glowed on her face, and in her eyes was the reflection of festivity of colors.

During this time, there lived a sentient *being* named Bodhi, who was like a big misty tree, laden with fruits, in a dry desert that travelers hoped to find refuge beneath, and satiate their hunger.

Bodhi was born with a magical virtue; anything that came close would reveal itself bare and bold effortlessly.

His soul was soaked in the bliss of oneness, and his skin breathed cosmic brilliance. His calm smile was like soft music echoed around the deep unknown valleys.

He lived like a wild and unknown native flower of springtime and adorned the garden of life with his profound grace.

One beautiful day, he was lying on a lush green grass bed next to the silver river and was watching the birds flying above, in the bright blue sky, and listening to the music of the tepid wind.

Suddenly, a tardy breeze swam from the east and ear-cuffed him. It carried a piercing but humble melody of hazy hopes, agony, and holiness.

The pain-filled euphony sank to the bottom of Bodhi's spirit and transformed his cosmic consciousness to earthly compassion.

The agony solidified his compassion into an intention to heal and free those holy *beings* living in bondage.

On the next tick of time, Bodhi stood, and holding the reins of the melodious chant, galloped eastward a great distance.

After several days and nights, he reached the fount of these ceremonial anthems.

Bodhi was surprised to realize that it was a shrine that many looked upon for healing their earthly and ethereal wounds.

He found that it was a short-range of three beautiful dwarf caves that radiated those obscure feelings.

Although the entrance to the small knoll was well below Bodhi's height, the weight of his compassion made him curl inward, and he crawled into the first cave.

It was dusky and silent inside, and a dim ray of white light shone from the center of the cave.

He saw a slouched plant with a curved spine that faced the only chink in the cave from where the light leaked down.

Bodhi's presence increased the tranquility of the cave, and the plant, thinking him a pilgrim, offered a warm welcome, and said, "O Bodhi, your immense calmness is like white clouds swimming in the blue sky of summer. You are most welcome in my cave."

The plant turned toward the slit of light and continued its prayer. Murmured the plant to the light, "O lamp of my life, without you I am nothing. Your existence is my existence, and you are the most beautiful shape of light. You are the only source of light in the whole cosmos."

Bodhi asked this plant, "What are you doing, and what happened to your spine?"

The plant replied, "Since my birth, I am naturally bent pulled toward this cast of light, which gives me life energy. It is my savior. I face its direction and live by it. Thus, I pay my homage out of love and respect."

Bodhi sensed an earnest heart filled with the pain of ignorance in its unnatural form, and replied, "I see your real hunger and pristine longing for the light, in your spirit, but it is wrapped in a cynical faith for its form.

"For years, you have seen the light through a groove, which has created an image of itself in you and blurred your sagacity to discriminate this image from the light. Light is flowing through the image, but the image itself is not the light.

"Your prayer and feelings of love took the shape of the groove from which light falls on your eyes and made you blind to anything new.

"Your craving for this cave's crack has twisted your face toward the crack and bent your spine, which should otherwise grow upward, naturally.

"Unknown to you, your body and mind have become habituated to the pain caused by this unnatural growth.

"Sadly, your faith has shaped your body into the shape of this crack and has blinded you to your real roots, which channel energy from within, in you.

"You must trust your strong roots to demolish the walls of this cave and free yourself from the bondage of blindness."

Bodhi's words hammered the plant to its core, and a current of anger throbbed in it as if a hidden fever rose to its skin.

The plant pointed at Bodhi with its thorns and said, "This crevice is the face of my God and source of my life, and its benediction is evident in me being a living thing.

"O Bodhi, you blemish the sacredness of my cave with your sordid tongue. You are an unworthy guest who is not welcomed anymore. Go away at once, and never return."

Bodhi murmured as if reciting some secret scriptures that others could feel but not hear, "I feel pity of your burdened and unnatural life. I must liberate you."

Having spoken, Bodhi uncurled himself, opened his long arms, and stood up.

The cave shattered as if a giant tree penetrated its strong roots and branches into the walls. This caused the cave to break and blend in the soil.

The plant was too petrified to leave a long life of darkness and searched for its hole of dim light. Unable to find its hole of dim light, it cried, "Look what you have done to me. I have no more purpose and guidance in my life. In which direction should I bow down? You have broken my image of light and my lamp of life."

Bodhi smiled, and words fell from his mouth as if angels appeared from the open doors of heaven: "The direction you attained in your cave was mere an alley between constraints; thus, I have not broken your life source, but rather, its restrictions.

"Living naturally is your essence and purpose of life. You must live what you are natively made for, neither less nor more."

The plant felt that its trunk no longer carried a tendency to bend in a distinct direction and rose to its natural height.

Thereupon, Bodhi realized that it was time for him to move on; he again coiled himself to enter the second cave.

This cave was shining brighter than the previous one and had several holes and cracks.

Bodhi saw an old plant that looked intelligent, broad, and hardworking, but it was crooked with many knots and bends.

Bodhi asked, "O thoughtful *being*, what do you do here in this cave, and why do you have so many deformities?"

The plant replied, "O Bodhi, your wisdom captures my being, and brightens this cave. You are most welcome here.

"I no longer bear the burden of following one lamp, and I understand that there are many forms and paths of light.

"I attained immense knowledge, and am known to various sources, and can drink through various mouths to quench my thirst.

"I walk on many paths and look upon many provenances. Some days I grow this way to pay homage and then turn and grow that way and then another.

"The bends on my body are not deformities; rather, they tell the story of paths known to me and make me feel immensely proud."

Hearing this self-pleasing talk, Bodhi uttered, "O crooked plant, although you look intelligent, your toil is inane and barren.

"It breeds ugly warps and turmoil in your being. You must annul this tendency of impotent effort."

The plant became furious as if somebody had cut the veins, supplying the blood to its heart, and looked upon Bodhi as a heinous being.

It replied, "O Bodhi, your petty wisdom cannot fathom the sweat of my efforts. None in this sacred site is comparable to me in the extent of knowledge.

"Go away at once with your lumpish advice."

Bodhi understood that throwing light on eyes blinded by argument- based knowledge would be of no avail. Let the strong hand of action reveal the truth.

Thus, Bodhi uncoiled himself and straightened his gigantic body until thin cracks widened, and with a sudden clap, the cave collapsed.

The second plant bawled, "O treacherous being, you have ruined my pride of knowledge and bulldozed my effort to come this far. This nonexistence of knowledge makes me dizzy."

Bodhi replied, "O old scholar plant, your expanse of knowledge was not of light, but the paths born out of strictures of the cave. Knowing light is true wisdom, and knowledge of paths is as false as your pilgrimage cave in itself.

"Before, you were king of this poor castle of knowledge. Today you are a wildflower of rich existence.

"Let this false knowledge of paths leave, instead experience the unfiltered light that feeds you from all directions and let you grow, naturally."

Thus, the plant realized that the false pride had faded, and the knots in its body melted and loosened its rigidity.

The plant said to itself, though each path shows light, the followership of anyone is meaningless since the true nature of light belongs to none. Bodhi's heart was still recycling the agony of plants into compassion.

He looked around for the third cave.

He then compacted himself again and entered the third cave.

A gruesome shock jolted him. The cave beamed with several rays of light and was full of noise, chaos, and conflict.

This view was very different from the previous caves; earlier, the plants were in bondages of selfdom, but here, the tendency was to dominate or be dominated by other plants.

This cave had many plants and many chinks, and each one struggled to reach its destination.

Bodhi dragged himself to the center of the cave and screamed, "O defilers of the holy shrine, what are you doing, and what is the conflict for?"

One of the plants replied, "I grew facing the oldest hole of light in the cave. Therefore, it surpasses everybody else and shall be worshiped by all."

A second plant replied, "I grew facing the crack that has given the light to many plants in this cave. Therefore, mine is superior."

And a third plant said, "I grew facing the slit that was the last in the lineage of all sacred cracks. Therefore, it has a fresh beam of light and is thus superior to others."

A fourth plant, who was facing a crack on the lower side of the cave, said, "Others try to reach their lamps, but I can touch the source of my light. Therefore, others are merely followers, and I have reached."

And many more plants argued the excellence of their cracks above the others.

This negativity and conflict sucked Bodhi's energy, and he failed to reconcile the shoddy minds.

He mustered his remaining energy and stood up to break the cave. The moment the cave broke, all comparisons evaporated. Many plants were happy to see the light as one source for all, but a few who were used to gain strength by making others feel small were sad.

At this moment, Bodhi's heart also became light, and he stood tall above the highest bough of plants.

Thus, spoke Bodhi, "Those plants which are in bondage to one path and deny clarity, live unnatural lives. And, those who are believers of the many paths live in the confusion of knowledge. And, those who live by comparisons to prove their paths live in fiction and conflict."

O Beloved, any direction is unnatural because existence has no direction. So, live with it as it is, naked and natural, realizing that layers are seasonal only.

Jyotish and the City of Shadows

Human ideologies are like shadows.
We create shadows, these shadows fight, and real humans suffer.
Sadly, we humans have collectively agreed
to live in the darkness of our shadows.

Prelude

Any obstruction in the path of light creates a shadow in the shape of the obstruction. Our consciousness is a kind of inner light that gets obstructed by our self-hood, and we project our consciousness in the shape of our self-hood in the outer world. This self-hood is an aggregation of ideologies and images we wear upon us.

Our ability to ideate is magical in comparison to any other species, and we have used and abused it to create countless ideologies in terms of religious, social, economical, and national frameworks. Humanity has become a hairball of doctored ideologies, and these ideologies follow us like shadows. These shadows make up our day-to-day realities, and we live by them. Moreover, our default mode of connection with other *beings* is through ideologies. Traditions and cultures make sure that we continue to hand over these shadows to our next generations. It feels like we are not born on planet earth, moving in the cosmic ocean, but born in the world of ideological ponds who meet with each other through the cracks of the earth in between.

We live in a large ideological network. And, in our day to day relationships, mostly we do not love or hate each other; rather, we love or hate our ideologies. This has severely impacted the entire humanity, more negatively than positively.

For example, India and Pakistan are two nations created in the past by leaders of the time. A large number of humans hate each other just because they are born on two sides of this made-up border. Consequently, this made-up image of self-hood has murdered so many human beings. There is no reason for animosity apart from ideological differences. Religions, caste, class, skin colors, sports, economy, and so on are the same way. The result is a judgmental mindset, inequality, confusion, insecurity, wars, suppressions, violence, and many more. Thus, the whole earth has become a collective society of shadows that relish in this ideology-bound shadow consciousness.

The list is too long where ideologies have obstructed a deep connection of one human to another. Our sense of belongingness is the result of a very complicated ideological network. Look around, and you will rarely meet a human *being* with a free consciousness. We walk wrapped in our ideologies as we walk with our clothes. This is an enormous burden on human consciousness.

Sadly, when shadows collide, they create suffering in innumerable ways for real human beings holding them. Real humans suffer from mythological shadows. In this world, human suffering is real, but its cause may be unreal, mainly when ideologies cause suffering.

Let's ask ourselves, can we think of a culture where we can make these ideologies powerless or secondary? It can be a dream only, but what stops us from evolving out of this ideological jacket? If a thing can be made, can we not un-make of re-make it?

Some people argue that ideologies are essential because, without them, a human being is an animal inside. Due to these massive arrangements, we are able to suppress our animal inside. Therefore, we cannot remove these ideologies. It is a very sad self-conception that we are deploying these ideologies to hold our animal behavior inside. Instead, we can use human intelligence to transform into conscious *being*s. It would take a cultural shift at a large scale because if a few insightful people do it, then this will be suppressed sooner or later.

This short story elaborates on this aspect of evolution, wherein this world is a world of shadows, and blind attachment to these ideologies causes enormous suffering in the world. And, entire society has forgotten that they are real humans, and live only as shadows. Somehow one person gets insight into this shadow based suffering and comes out of shadows. Then, he wanders with this light for some time in the world, but soon he becomes an enemy of other shadows and gets killed by them.

Poem

Jyotish was the firstborn and was created out of light and space. Thereupon he witnessed the creation of other *beings*.

He lived as a white, luminous constellation, and the luster of his light could fade out the milky way in the cosmic ocean.

And being a sky wanderer, he loved to explore the evolution of life- forms on various celestial objects floating in the cosmos.

Once, he heard about the tiny City of Shadows, and its magical evolution, from other space travelers. The City of Shadows was several light-years away from Jyotish.

But the desire to see the city moved him in its direction toward the dark matter.

For eons, he swam in the galactic river, passing amazing galaxies, and many clusters of stars and planets.

And upon getting closer to the city, he diluted himself into the ether to remain hidden in a faint form. Thereupon he entered the City of Shadows.

As he stepped in, he saw two dark and hefty shadows were fighting to slay each other, surrounded by hundreds of other shadows cheering loudly.

Jyotish was jolted and looked around with curiosity; one enthusiast told him that this was a sport of strength and success. And the declaration of victory over another was the way to enrich the moments of their lives.

Shocked, Jyotish said to himself, "Why is it that the silent tears of one would be loud laughter of the other? Were you not created to enjoy harmony rather than extract joy from the defeat of an enemy?" He then sought a secluded alley away from the crowd.

He moved in the dark for a while until he heard some shrieking noises fuming out from the house at the corner of a street, and followed it.

Two shadows were quarreling and accusing each other, an awful wife and husband. Their feelings were full of regret and remorse upon remembering their marital lock.

And a thought occurred to Jyotish: "Were you not created as man and woman to bear joy and love for each other? In the name of 'social unit,' you evolved into roles of husband and wife and created a mesh of rotten relations." And he moved on.

After that, he saw a very serene and peaceful queue of shadows coming out of a temple.

Upon asking, he was told, "The God who lives here washes their sins and purges the pain in exchange for a cup of devotion. And it is better than any other god in the city."

Jyotish thought, "Doesn't God breathe through you anymore? Since when has devotion become a utility to afford?"

After that, he saw copious, richly decorated shadows walking over shadows crippled in the hell of poverty.

Jyotish uttered to himself in sorrow, "Were you all not created with one mouth and one belly? How did you become polarized between hoarding and hundreds of hunger?" And he moved toward the periphery of the city.

He then saw a dark shadow followed by a pack of angry armored shadows with flags and symbols. They were marching in unison toward the south.

Upon being asked, one of them said, "Tonight we will destroy the south city, their commander, and their army."

Jyotish froze at the sight of the destruction of beings, and murmured, "Are you not fruits of the same soil? How did you divide the soil for the love of flags and create ordinances for wars?"

Seeing enough of the evolution of the shadows, Jyotish moved toward the center, where the leaders and builders of the society were busy writing the laws of evolution.

As he reached nearby the center, the shadows grew denser and darker.

Women and men of all classes were consumed in the eclipse. Gloomy, uncertain images were surfing on their faces.

Unbearable were the shadows. Thus, Jyotish broke his silence and asked them the cause of their emergence and darkness.

Jyotish said in a loud voice, "Who has cursed this city with the misery and bondage of shadows? And why have you accepted this shelter of the murk?"

On hearing the outcry, a responsible older man's shadow, with puffed, mature eyes, came out through the layers of the umbra.

And with a qualm gesture, he looked upon Jyotish, but with a potent tongue, he spoke the truth known to him that he had held upon for ages.

"O Cosmic traveler, we welcome you to our city. We value our shadows and invest in their existence for the love of purposeful arrangements, more than the love for freedom and creativity.

"Unfortunately, the city has forgotten its birthmarks, and therefore invented the shadows in the form of religions, societies, commerce, and nations in the name of convenience and order.

"We realize that we suffer from their miseries, but these shadows fill our emptiness with a purpose, and save us from an old yet deep and unanswered question about our "origin and becoming."

"Are we here by choice of craftsmanship or by chance of combinations? This is an ageless debate that we fail to solve, and this is as old as the city itself.

"If it was by choice of some almighty craftsman, then why was the imperfection chosen to make us suffer this life of misery, which pushes us always to perfect ourselves? From animals to humans and from humans to gods.

"And if it was by chance, then this orphan life goes astray by the guilt of our insignificance and meaninglessness. And, then the only thing which matters to us, is pleasures of our senses and strong power over others. So, why shouldn't we create selfish meanings and modes for daily living?

"Was our "becoming" a dot on the dice or an arrow on the bow? And which is of higher value, hope or reason?"

"This very question has divided the time into cause and effect, and nature into natural and supernatural, and has split our souls into microcosm and macrocosm. It divorced the action from its result, with blades of will or fate.

"Our egos love the path of power and thus long for this division— betwixt the being and the world.

"Therefore, we created purpose, perfection, and meaning through shadows of religions, commerce, societies, and nations."

After this long commentary, followed by an esoteric silence, the old man looked upon Jyotish, and asked,

"You are a stranger in our city and behold the secrets of creation. Speak to us the truth and meaning of our *being*."

Hearing this, Jyotish looked at the darkness all around and felt the pain. Instantly, all the sufferings this city had experienced in the past appeared before his eyes.

Said Jyotish to the Oldman, "O Beloved curious one. With all honesty, I speak what I see without any bias for the ghosts of your city.

"I only know what I see here and speak only what I know. So, carve a door in your heart for me to enter.

"These eyes see in this city, deep darkness, what cannot be erased by conflict and competition.

"And the shadows achieve nothing, to ease their pain and suffering by this.

"Although there is a marvelous creation of your thoughts in the shapes of religions, societies, commerce, and nationhood, they are the prime sources of darkness.

"Also, I see that utilitarian desires impregnated your mind, and naturally, the result is another form of utility.

"This utilitarian approach accumulates suppressed desires as another form of utility.

"You are bound to see life more rigid, complicated, and conflicted in those beings wherever these colors are dark—be it clergy, leaders, gamers, aristocrats, or politicians.

"You have evolved into systems of yourself, but the "self" remains un- evolved. The evolution of "self" starts with the involution as the first gate.

"The real reason for your non-resolution is that you are trying to find solutions for darkness using another form of darkness.

"And all your complicated questions are just simple outcomes of same darkness; it is not even multicolored. It is only different in degrees of dark shades.

"Because all questions are born out of the same source, there is no single form wise enough to answer the uneasy being.

"Must you evolve the consciousness upward and stop finding remedies of solace in these shades? All are merely relative illusions of one another and are unreal.

"You have switched the gear of life in the utility of things around and entirely forgotten to realize the neutrality of *being*.

"Sensing the neutral "self" enables the cognition with an awareness that the feeling, remembering, and thinking are byproducts of *knowing* and not the *knowing* itself. Thus, you can use these faculties in such a way that understanding of the world is empty of dark shadows. You must meditate to arrange "yourself" rather than things belonging to you.

"But these religions, societies, groups, commerce, and nations are made in such a way that your spirit is not left with any door but a puzzling way of life. In this design, you belong to them. Thus you are tailored by them.

"Hence, there is so much noise outside and inside the *being* for subsistence.

"Honestly, there are no real answers, as your questions are unreal and born out of shadows. The answers to all questions of dreaming are by awakening, instead of seeking them in the dreams while asleep.

"Like a drunk artist who decorates herself looking in the mirror but forgets her real self and starts decorating the image in the mirror, so does slight movement bring imbalance between the image in the mirror and the ornaments.

"And you may ask if this imbalance is by choice or by chance. A *being* untouched by this hallucination can say clearly that you are decorating the images and not your real "self." Hence, you experience the misery of meaninglessness in spite of your enormous efforts.

"Other illusions can not answer the questions born out of illusions; the only doorway is the death of illusion.

"A neutral consciousness is free to move. Hence, it is liberated out of its own jacket of ideologies.

"This allows for the freedom to move in other forms of real-life, be its existence, higher potential of existence, or continuously interacting with one another.

"From here, you see that life is not a dichotomy of chance or choice.

"So, the questioner is real, but questions are unreal."

Thereupon, all questions of the old man transformed into one question, and he asked, "What is to be done or undone to know the neutral?"

Jyotish replied, "When the *being* sees the utter meaninglessness of these shades and intends to come out of all of them at once, and not one by one, the real question emerges in life and hence gathers the potential to change the reality of consciousness by realizing it at its root level and cause of its misery to be burnt.

"Like how a paper spread on the ground in sunlight could only become warm, if someone brings a lens to focus the sun's rays on it, it will burn like fire.

"Similarly, the churning of shadows could bring some warm agitation around it, but it can never be a light unto itself."

Jyotish then flew into the old man through the door in his heart and transformed him into a mist of light.

The old man cast no more shadows and walked like a natural flame. Seeing this magic of liberation from shadows, both rejoiced in the light of life.

Jyotish then left the city with a smile and went farther and farther into the galactic river through the milky way.

As he moved, his faint form transformed into a sharp, dazzling form of light and space but with an unknown sweet attachment with a friend he left behind.

Back in the city of shadows, the old man started sharing the wisdom he had attained, with others.

A few hundred years passed by, and Jyotish's attachment took the form of a desire to revisit the city of shadows and meet his old friend.

And he flew in its direction, already known to him, passing galaxies and the milky way.

Upon reaching the borders of the city, which was now a territory, unexpectedly, he found it intensely dark and much disturbed than before.

Immediately he asked about his old friend, and somebody told him the tragic end of his friend.

Jyotish was taken to the center of the city, where he saw a colossal statue of his friend.

The shadows gathered around Jyotish and said, "after you left, the old man moved within the city, and wherever he went, he brought trouble with him for shadows. In his presence, the shadows started shrinking and felt distracted from their purpose and living.

"He became a threat to the constitution of our city.

"Therefore, it was decided that on the day of the eclipse, when the stars shut their eyes, the mist of light would be killed.

"He was brought to the center of the city and buried deep under the weight of shadows until no trace remained.

"But we gave his life a purpose and meaning and created his giant dark tomb at the same place.

"Now he casts countless shadows and is a friend of the city again, and he is our torchbearer for deeper quests of life.

"It is best that he lives peacefully below the city while we live above the city with our purpose and missions alive.

"But, the mist of light buried beneath the ground has cast myriad shadows above and haunts us with a question: Is it a choice of super or the chance of natural events?

"Would you know the answer, Jyotish?" asked the shadows in excitement.

Hearing this, Jyotish looked around the miserable darkness and left the city at once without answering or looking back. As he moved away, he sensed that he was also liberated from his sweet attachment to the enlightened old friend.

And that was the last journey of Jyotish to the city of Shadows.

The Hypocrite's Village

I am not what you think I am.
You are not what you show you are.
We are not what we believe we are.
Hypocrisy is the biggest deception that human society nurtures.

Prelude

He who restrains his organs of action but continues in
his mind to brood over the objects of sense,
whose nature is deluded, is said to be a hypocrite
(a man of false conduct).

- The Bhagavad Gita, Chapter 3 Verse 6

The days and nights of a hypocrite's life go in revealing and concealing identities for the approval of others. They are burnt much faster with the fuel of comparison and jealousy.

Hypocritical thinking knits a complex network in your objective awareness. You live confused, in conflict, and with self-denial. Your one hand, compresses the real *You* inside, and the other hand, expresses an unreal of *you* outside. This push and pull, make life tensed, and tiring. It begins with small manageable lies, but becomes so addictive that your mind gets accustomed to this tension, and enjoys living as a habitual hypocrite. It can be found in all ages after the birth of social identity. It changes by levels of social standards and matures over time. For example, it is found more often in intellectuals, religious leaders, celebrities, wealthy people, political leaders, and so on. Hypocrisy is everywhere, in religions, charity, corporations, social groups, social media, politics, family, education, health care, and so on. It's a rampant disease; almost everyone is pretending to be someone else to the other. Aren't we living in a strange human world? But why is it so widespread? And why is it so easy to be a hypocrite?

Over time, with experience and practice, one becomes an expert hypocrite. We mimic and learn it from each other, and differ in degrees only. We do not need a school or specialized curriculum for its training; any society by its comparative design and standards promotes a culture of hypocrisy. It makes it easy to learn and allows for gaining expertise. Living in this world design is like "on the job training" to become a hypocrite.

We become expert hypocrites due to its wide variety of application scenarios. Almost every form of action we connect in the world can reinforce it. It can be exercised through our physical appearances, all five physical senses, and intellect. For example, *our physical appearance* can be elusive via facial makeup, expressions, clothes, body art, body language, style of walking, eating, moving, and so on. During *touch*, one can shake hands, give hugs, or kiss, but hate internally. While *speaking*, one can modulate tones, pitch, talking points, but mean differently. Via *smell*, one can pretend to like good smells, but dislike internally. Upon *hearing*, one can hear and pretend not to hear or something else. While *eating*, one can pretend the food to be tasty but will never want to eat it. And when thinking *intellectually*, one can copy and supply thoughts to pretend someone else.

No wonder, without teaching, everybody is taught the power of hypocrisy.

Although, if we can make a similar culture for conscious living, the entire humanity can become consciously awake without any teacher or teaching. Well, it's a wishful dream for now.

The above-said applications are merely doors to allow hypocrisy, but the real reasons are deep down in the *being's* psychology. It is rooted in the formation of *social identity or ego*. Our ego is composed of superiority or inferiority complexes. And, hypocrisy is *becoming* of these complexes into multiple and more advanced versions. How?

A hypocrite splits identity for the outer world to achieve a specific outcome upon social interaction. This can be due to insecurity, fear, acceptance, approval, or to gain some benefits.

For example, a person who is from a minority class or poverty, when joining a club of majority class, or wealthy people, will try to show superiority. A leader who needs votes from the poor social class will try to show inferior behaviors. A religious person will try to pretend of great sacrifices to gain respect, and so on. In all cases, identity gets split into outer and inner forms. Although all identities are made up of a localized social structure and are unreal, to begin with, the problem is a little bit deeper and clumsy. Why so? Let's look at the typical life of human beings in the modern world. A regular person has a *home identity*. They live in a home with a husband or wife, kids, parents, or siblings. An *office identity* is when they go to the office to work with peers, higher up leaders, or a team. *Religious identity* refers to those who attend church or temple with followers or preachers. *Political identity* refers to one who believes in one party to come into power. *Sports identity* is for those who enjoy the winning of the favorite team over another. *Social identity* shows a happy- go- lucky image on social media and publicity, and so on.

Each instance shows a person with an identity complex. It looks like your ego complex is a wallet of many IDs. Who are you in these identities? How do you manage the plural identity vs. your singular entity? We live life not as individuals but as compounds of IDs.

Hypocrisy takes this psychological problem of your ego-collage to the next level upon social interaction. The aggregate of identities gets further split to showcase a false identity on top of an already made- up identity. In-home, a husband shows off to be superior to the wife, in-office you project superiority over peers, in a church, you're most humble, in politics you must show assertiveness, in sports you show up as an aggressive fan, and on social media, you want to be the most liked person. Isn't it so?

An identity is a vehicle to create feelings in us. It can be pleasurable or painful based on the experience of that identity. A hypocritical identity also becomes a vehicle to produce feelings— from very pleasurable to extremely un-pleasurable feelings, either in oneself or others. One end of the spectrum could be pretentious praises, greetings, and another end could be betrayal or backstabbing.

It's a massive effort to manage your identities in one life. Are you not fed up of this identity business? How can you realize the true "indivisible" intention of your *being*? You spend so much psychic energy managing tensed layers and the weight of these identities, so your efforts are always divided into identities, and you feel meaningless inside.

Perhaps this is the reason that deep hypocrites fear to self-reflect. They need a lonely place and a blame-free mirror to uncover themselves, to see "who am I," beneath these identities. If not, then they rather die in self-deception than self-reflection. Many don't even care about it and want to live hidden and camouflaged from the world. They find escapes from themselves in the form of entertainment and addiction, where they can forget the internal conflict due to hypocrisy.

Hypocrisy has become an important social skill. But, we are hypocrites for hypocrisy itself, because internally one feels proud to get things done hook or by crook, but openly it is a taboo. Look at a simple interesting fact; every day, we hear in the news about religious or political leaders and things they have done wrong. Thus, we enjoy making hateful comments on them, but the same thing we maybe doing ourselves secretly. In other words, we allow our hypocritical actions internally, but we criticize others outwardly for the same behavior. Most definitely, we do not want our hypocrisy to be caught by others. So, we are hypocrites about hypocrisy itself.

If you analytically inquire about a hypocrite self, you will find that behind all the lies out of which a hypocrite's life is evolved, the "original lie" would always be to himself or herself. One cannot lie to others without lying to himself or herself. Hence, in this world, people think that they are smart and can deceive others, but the root is always self- deception. It looks convoluted, but it's true.

One wonders and can argue, hypocrisy is a social issue. Why does a person need to understand it for self-exploration, which is an individual's journey?

Yes, it is a social problem. Hypocrisy needs a womb of "you vs. me" to take birth, but this topic is essential for indirect reasons more than the direct reasons for self-inquiry. We live in a complicated world and need to be practically cautious of what is to be excluded and included for self-exploration. There are three main reasons to understand hypocrisy and precautions to avoid it. Firstly, it creates false identities that delude a *being* by its debris of thinking, sensing, and feelings; one needs to clear it up by taking self-awareness as a surgical task. Secondly, for practical reasons, you are not living in isolation; therefore, alertness and discipline are essential to remaining original, and anything plastic needs to be recycled out. And, thirdly, a very subtle reason is that self-awareness expands the psyche to be all-inclusive and universal, whereas hypocrisy contracts the psyche because a *being* wants to hide reality inside. This contradiction is very unhealthy for self-exploration.

This short story examines the life of a hypocrite who has realized the pain of it and is looking for a lonely opportunity to come out of his social masks. He wants to live and breathe free. This poem suggests a schema to get rid of the hypocritical mind. Obviously, the starting step is to realize the pain of hypocrisy; thereupon decide to transform, follow the innocence and openness, be receptive of truth and let the hypocrite- self die out to allow the birth of originality, naturally. Coercion, guilt, and suppression of hypocritical self are not solutions.

Also, this poem elaborates on the importance of innocence and directness over hypocritical crookedness.

HONESTY
IS
BEST POLICY
SCHOOL
HEALTH CENTRE
PARLIAMENT

Poem

Today, the first ray of the rising sun kissed my forehead and pushed me out of the edges of my sleep.

All the villagers have gone out for the carnival feast, but I desire to keep the carnal fast and look after my starving soul.

I have been waiting for this day for ages, as I have been living betwixt the thresholds of inner rage and outer bondage.

I remembered my soul-tearing agony, concealed under my uptight and uptown persona that I uphold and exhibit in the village.

But today, I want from the depth of my heart to breathe through the blisters of my pus-ridden soul and inhale the fresh air.

As I gaze out of my window into the village to see, all homes are abandoned, and the market is closed, and no visitor is expected.

Only the tepid wind is blowing the sand of empty streets, and ringing the bells of the barren temple.

Thus, I undrape myself and walk naked in the streets of the village, fearlessly.

I stroll in the streets and pass through the temple, village assembly, market, school, and the court.

I pause before them, one by one, to pay homage and furl through the memories of my life spent there.

Suddenly, I hear a giggling coming from a side alley, and as nobody should have been in the village today, I am filled with surprise and follow the sound.

A little later, in an open space, under the sunshine, I see an innocent young child with clear eyes, radiant skin, and clattering laughter standing before me.

As soon as he sees me, he gets scared and asks, "Who are you? You look familiar. Where have I seen you before? And why are you so ugly and full of disease and disgust?"

I get stunned and surprised by the directness of his questions, and for an unknown reason, I feel obliged to answer and say,

"O little bundle of innocence and fresh vigor, I am like a hybrid of snake and bee, who scatters honey to seek approval of others, although my actions secretly secrete the poison from the hidden limbs in my *being.* "And I am like an aloof house inhabited by a timid ghost, whose walls are eaten by termites of endless lies, though it is painted outside

with shiny steel to uphold the pride.

"And I am like an oafish thief, who earnestly waits for the gloom, to befriend the villager's meekness and nab their belongings—but I keep them in a torn bag and do not realize, until I enter my house, that I am still empty inside and unfulfilled.

"In this village, strange is my worth and use. The villagers look upon me as a torchbearer, until I am a stranger to them, and once I am known, they enjoy hating me. But they shelter me in the shrine of their own hearts and protect me from others, and they keep me knowingly unknown to themselves.

"O little seer of purity, you are right that you have seen me because only your eyes are capable of recognizing me, as others are prejudiced by their envious desire to be *me.*

"You have seen me as a religious master who sits on lofty altars and is wrapped in gaudy gowns, delivering sermons to perfect the human into God, but my actions are fruits of my hidden subhuman desires.

"And you have seen me as a disciple who imitates angels and behaves as a 'perfected one' to seek approval and rewards from the crowd outside, but when I'm lonely, my inner crowd of demons is liberated, like the water who attains the shape and size of the vessel it belongs to; until the moment arrives when the vessel is broken, which then follows the gravity of its true weight.

"And you have seen me as a religious worshipper who believes in omniscience and the non-locality of the divine, but I bind faith and action for a chosen venue of worship and seek security in it.

"And you have seen me like a king who sits on the tall throne of trust, untouched by hands of fear and favor, but I bend down under the weight of my greed, and prefer crookedness over righteousness.

"And you have seen me as a lawmaker who has crafted the force of constitution for the people to abide and carefully maintained the hidden ways to bend it, for my unlawful desires.

"You have seen me as an endorsed healer who vows for health, service, and the sympathy for others, though my spirit professes the merchandise of sickness and the actions of a parasite.

"You have seen me as an acclaimed poet whose humble pen is filled with the ink of art, beauty, and love, although the body is filled with the blood of forgery, jealousy, and vainglory.

"You have seen me in a scientist, who exhibits a passionate curiosity to experiment and learn the unknown nature of things around, although my hands selectively touch the gilded gadgets only.

"You have seen me like an esteemed social worker who promises to polish individuals as diamonds and build a sparkling society, although I craft heavy norms to cripple individuals and create flocks. My piggish desires move the fulcrum between 'individuals for society' or 'society for individuals,' as one's weakness is the strength of another.

"This infectious sickness, fettered by my own beliefs and habits, has domesticated me for a long time.

"The lake of my soul is polluted by egregious debris of my heinous actions, from which, once, I wished to fill up the cup of virtues and serve others.

"But I let my wandering desires polish the mask of made-up beliefs and left my soul uncared and unclean.

"In truth, I am always short in my deeds when compared to my image. "In short, I am a hypocrite, and this is my village."

Then, I pause my speech of vexed memories and walk a little closer to say, "O little prodigious shiny stream.

"Your presence is creating eddies in my heart like bubbles in stagnant water. Who are you?"

Thereupon, the little one cries in pain and says, "O hypocrite, your sickness has impaired your memory, and you have forgotten me.

"I am the freshness of spirit spread by the wings of freedom.

"And I am the flower of innocence that germinates in the womb of a mother and perfumes the childhood.

"Ye have cut me off from thyself for thy love of filth. Since then, I have roamed in the streets of the village."

Then I say, "O little recluse; many mansions are entitled to me, whose decorated doors welcome you. You should not hesitate to adopt the lavish gifts of this village."

The little one says in a composed voice, "O ignorant hypocrite, could freshness breathe through the soil of stink? Similarly, ye and I cannot coexist.

"Must thee die now and let the spirit be born again and live at ease in light of innocence? Remember the oldest wisdom of sages to become *dvija* (twiceborn)."

I look at the village and then to my whimpering soul, and for the first time in my life, my head sinks into my heart.

And with the silent speech of my swollen eyes, I invite the little angel of death to infuse a new life and liberate me.

Thereupon, the sharp light of innocence pierces my heart, and my crippled soul is unburdened, and peace prevails, and deep sleep comes upon me.

When I awake, I am fresh as a flower and light like air, when I walk into the village again, uncaring of my nakedness.

I see that the villagers are returning. They had been looking for me in the temple, the courthouse, and everywhere, where I was commonly found.

I say to myself, I wish I could tell them the secret that the hypocrite is dead now, and another secret—that nature never takes anything until it gives back.

Now I exist as an incense of innocence, and spontaneity, and in ordinary abundance.

Then, days passed by, and the villagers forgot me in any extraordinary form.

Now I dwell as a perfume in the simple hearts of friends who hold each other in times of turbulence.

And I dwell as a religious master who pours his unseen wisdom in a disciple, not to make a follower—nay, a master—and magically get filled up again to fill others tirelessly.

And I dwell as a worshipper whose devotion is divine, and any object where the devotion is fixed becomes a temple.

And I dwell as a healer who is uneased by the diseased nearby, and whose work of restoration is an art of devotion.

And I dwell as a king who cut part of his powerful self to make the weak, strong.

I live in all ordinary actions sprouted in beingness and directed outside, unhindered, and transparent and dead to any extraordinary maze games made by walls of a belief that play with the self.

O Beloved,

Beware, as the soil of the mind is clever enough to reform into a house of hypocrisy, and it will defend the cunning actions outside.

Rather live this life happily here and now by enjoying togetherness through the doors of the six senses, and let the colorless consciousness efface it every time. Let happiness remain a virgin forever.

Dreams: Hidden Portal of Awareness

A dream is a creative sleep.
Only creativity can bring transformation, free from any obsession.

Prelude

The human mind is a wonderland. In a way, it is magical in designing experiences; close your eyes, and you can create a beautiful garden, magnificent castle, or tasty food in your mind, and immediately you feel good. Also, you can create hell in your mind by thinking the opposite.

Isn't it great to have such power of imagination and autosuggestion? But, this power also makes it very hard to decipher the real vs. unreal. Our imaginative faculty works in both—wakefulness and dream state. One is a volunteer, and the other is non-volunteer for most of us.

How do you know that the world is not your imagination? When you wake up in the morning, do you ask yourself, *Is this world real or imaginary?* Probably, you don't because others confirm your perception. For example, you see a tree, and your friends sees a tree and tells you the specifications, and you believe them. So, a collective validation becomes truth, and its repetition becomes the reality of daily life. What if your friend imagines as well under some universal laws of imagination in existence? Like, we commonly assume gravity is permanent for shared and practical reasons in day to day life, but it is also situational in existence. Therefore, it becomes really hard for those experiences which no one else can validate for you, how do you categorize them? For example, an immersive, meditative experience.

We all are experience seeking *beings*, and this world is our stage where we work, laugh, play, suffer, and experience, and we believe it is real, but the same can happen in a dream. In waking state, the role of "will" is supreme, and we experience the world while doing a task, whereas in dreams, "watching" is supreme, and we experience the world as a happening to us. In this happening, we can be doing as well, maybe in a passive role.

Truly, we know the world by happening of an experience to us. In this way, dreams are no way less important than wakefulness. Dreams are hidden portals of awareness and are our informers of intrinsic reality. Images in dreams are a response to processes involving our physical, emotional, and psychic levels of existence.

Thinking is like dreaming, but both occur in different modifications of consciousness. Therefore, we end up with a different quality of experience. Thinking uses primarily superficial consciousness and fetches information from the senses and the subconscious, depending upon how deep the level of thinking is. During thinking, our "will" takes a central role, and it is a well-coordinated effort to fetch information and associate images using logic. Whereas in cases of dreaming, the subconscious plays a vital role and brings up information to conscious levels. Because of this, the role of "will" is subdued, although imagination can occur in both modifications of consciousness.

Extreme experiences in life can create a response in the form of mental images. It can be a physical response or due to emotions. It can be the result of a deeper layer unknown to thinking mind. In any case, dreams are doors to deep-seated self-knowledge. For example, if we are hungry, then dreams of food are reasonable. Due to their connection to our subconscious, dreams are helpful portals to know ourselves.

Even after so much scientific advancement, we know very little about our dreams. Maybe everything is a continuous stream of dreams.

This short poem merely scratches the surface of dreams to inspire the reader not to overlook their importance in self-exploration. It also provides a short comparison between dreams and thinking. This poem indicates few types of dreams helpful in enhancing their understanding. Read it carefully and slowly, as dreams can be beneficial in knowing the deeper states of the mental framework.

Poem

O Beloved,
In the history of human life,
dreams are older than their thoughts.
They carry sagacious meaning
in their folds and compressed knots.

In this great lake of the mind,
the *thinking* is a recent kin
and works well for the trivial life,
like any other make-up skin.

But dreams are shy and introvert.
They wait for your attention and never assert.
While thoughts are bold and extrovert,
they need a network of memory and your volition to exert.

Dreams are knots between known and unknown,
and thoughts are linear ripples and are ego-borne.
Dreams flower in a receptive mind,
and thoughts develop in an active mind.

Dreams are born while you are awake or asleep.
They are the keyholes to the subconscious to peep.
Do not ignore the knowledge coming through them,
but filter wisely between their dirt and the gem.

Because not all dreams are equal,
few are deep, and most are dull.
Few are reactions to impressions deeply hiding in,
mostly are like residual desires of the day in a recycle bin.

To let your *being* live in bliss and fulfilled,
you must open the gates of your awareness field.
Let no dream remain hidden behind desires,
and awareness uncloaks them as perception fires.

A dream of this world is more figurative than conceptual
and the dream of "self" is more sensational than literal.
Deep but simple is the meaning of this dichotomy,
acutely aware of "self" versus the world in your dream anatomy.

The sensation of "self" is a heap of osmotic experiences,
betwixt the world and knowledge gained through senses.
Solidified ego superimposes on "self" and brings a sense of
possession, the absence of which breaks the subjective and
objective connection.

However, in dreams when the clutch of ego is weak,
the constituents of "self," and its patterns are open to leak.
Memory supplies the images to splice,
within which the dynamic image of "self" is one of the slices.

Ego-less state brings another type of dreams,
those are rare and independent of earthly osmotic streams.
Coming through the bridge of life's subtlest blueprint,
it confuses ego due to lack of its ownership imprint.

Let the *being* extract the message from inside,
which may confer meaning to this feckless life.
Without the ego, life is a continuous stream of calm consciousness,
and inner dreams bubble up in it, as a nonlocal projection
of omniscience.

It is unfortunate and unwise,
that modern man has accepted and applied
his ego to singularize and self-hypnotize,
and let it ignore the cues from inside, which can truly demystify.

O thought-driven soul,
take a vacation from thinking.
Subside your ego and watch it sinking.
Have no choice or conditions to bind your awareness,
and let your deepest repressions loosen up the beingness.

Let the vehicle of dreams help the soul
by unfolding the buried valleys into the whole,
and let the *being* be free from latent impressions,
to dance in the shine of truth, with naked expressions.

Section 3

Beyond the Being and Becoming

Do you know?
Who are you? &
What is your story? &
Are you beyond your story?

If,
Answer = 'No' Then,
Repeat.

— The truth algorithm

The Lonely Meditator and His Final Wish

The entire endeavor of meditation is to reveal what you really are.
In meditation, we declutter and declutch the mind
to allow pure consciousness to shine.

Prelude

*When the pot is broken, the space within it is absorbed
in the infinite space and becomes undifferentiated.
When the mind becomes pure, I do not perceive any difference
between the mind (being) and the Supreme Being.*

-Avadhut Gita (The song of free)- Dattatreya, Chapter 1, verse 31

Let's read a short story of Mr. Atoz (pronounced as *A.2.Zee*)
On a bright sunny day after lunch, Mr. Atoz is sitting on a bench in the corner of a beautiful park. In an elated mood, while listening to the faint giggles of neighborhood kids, playing in the park, he opens his favorite book of *wisdom-quotes* and starts reciting. After some time, he softly closes his eyes, places the book on his face as an eye-cover, and lies down on the bench to bathe in the warm daylight. Slowly, he starts sinking in a calm and cool lake of the mind.

All of a sudden, a screeching sound strikes his eardrums. Disturbed violently, his mind creates an image of a car as the source of this sound. Thereupon, his mind's eye zooms into the car and sees his wealthy neighbor's teenage son on the driver's seat. He starts cursing the teenager for driving rashly and honking all the time. His mind full of abuses erupts his mindless anger to the peak levels and compels him to kick the car hood. As a result, the frantic teenager runs the car over Mr. Atoz.

Trembling out of fear, Mr. Atoz falls off the bench on one side, and the book of *wisdom-quotes* drops on the other side. Shockingly, he opens the eyes to look around and sees the day is as beautiful as it was. But the bigger shock comes when he sees the neighbor's teenage son standing before him with a cup of water.

With a pang of hidden guilt in heart, and hindered gratitude in mind, Mr. Atoz says, "Thank you, son!" and drinks the cold water. He looks at his watch; only 10 mins were passed since he came into the park.

The teenager leaves him, but with a great lesson and a turning point in life.

Mr. Atoz wants to know the root cause of this illusion resulting in a painful experience. He wants to know the nature of experience, arising, living, and dying in his body-mind framework.

He sits alert on the bench and leaves the book of wisdom-quotes on the ground. Thereupon, reflects on the graph of his recent experiences vs. time.

In 10 minutes, Mr. Atoz experiences existential peace, amusement, irritation, anger, biases, guilt, and gratitude. One after another, he investigates the forms of experience from worldly to sensory to perceptual to emotional to feelings, and so on. The story of self-discovery continues.

Now, Mr. Atoz is a sincere meditator. So, let's leave him on his journey and put the spotlight on your life. Is it different from Mr. Atoz's experience graph? Or is it a much thicker scrapbook of experiences? This scrapbook is nothing but your life story.

What is experience? Each experience is a composition of various forms. Each form creates an impression of pleasurable, painful, or neutral feelings in our consciousness. Each impression produces a sense of identity associated with the forms. This association creates a sense of ownership. Thereupon, we end up concluding, I am this, or I am that. Isn't it very superficial?

Can we go beneath the painful and pleasurable feelings to realize our existential experience?

Let's use a word—*Meditation* as a systematic process of this fundamental realization. Many wise people have said that meditation is a process through which a *being* lives joyful, conscious, and connected with existential truth. One wonders, is this lucrative claim—a reality or a theory? Of course, to validate this hypothesis, we need to experiment with it sincerely. But first, we need to understand the nature of human experience—technically. Thereupon, we need to comprehend the underlying mechanics of mind in meditation, and how it alters the living experience—positively and practically.

As it can be very confusing to peel the onion of human experience, let's borrow few concepts from two ancient Indian philosophies, namely *Sankhya*, by Sage Kapil and *Yog-Darshan* by Sage Patanjali for a systematic understanding and save us from intellectual randomness. These ideas are about—Forms, Identity, Illusion, Consciousness, Prime Desire, Meditation, and their inter-relationships.

First, let's begin with defining a form. In simple terms, a form has a name and some unique attributes—qualitative and quantitative. Our body is also a form, made up of many inter-related forms—physical and mental, which are the building blocks of our perceptual reality. A short survey of these sub-forms can be helpful here.

The coverage of physical forms is comprised of billions of sensations, received via five major senses from the outer world. Every single moment we use one or more of these five doors of senses—sight, smell, touch, taste, and hearing, to consume raw information and perceive reality. This is how we perceive the world in terms of—distances, shapes, solidity, colors, odors, perfumes, textures, pressure, temperature, pain, sweetness, salty, sour, bitter, savory, and melodious sounds and noises. These senses are not interchangeable but integral to create perception. For example, taste and smell work together to conclude if food is delicious or not.

If it is too much to grasp, then hold on to your breath because the next level of mental forms is not only overwhelming but very complicated to comprehend. Let's start with its most simple and superficial forms, like ideas, concepts, and thoughts, which are a very small part of our consciousness but keep us engaged all day long in terms of language, nations, rituals, beliefs, and so on. The second types are of dreams, intuitions, and imaginations coming up from the sub-conscious floor in ways of artistic work, reflections, anticipations, and so on. The third type is feelings, emotions, and sensations, which inform us about hot, cold, pleasure, jealousy, anger, and so on. The fourth type is memories like short and long term, biological clock for sleep, appetite, time-sensitivity, cellular memory, deep conditioning, biases, and so on.

All physical forms are also transformed into mental forms for the experience to occur. In fact, the story of our living experience is a collage of mental images, and our mindset is an album made up of the association, differentiation, comparisons, classification, patterns, measurements, and prioritizations of experiences. Everyone wants to keep happy images and delete the sad ones, but it is not in our hands unless we go into the making of this album, which is the art of meditation. Let's talk about a few more concepts before exploring the meaning of meditation.

If a form is an object of our experience, then consciousness is the subjective field in which experience occurs. In its presence, the knowledge of forms occurs, like the light in which the world is seen.

Human consciousness is fundamentally pure and formless but gets modified when mixed with forms during an experience, and the power of mixing is such that *being* adopts the limitation and associated pain or pleasure of the form. No wonder our day is full of drama, and nights are full of dreams of the daily drama.

There is another very important side-effect of this intermixing of forms with consciousness occurs—a sense of self-identity. This sense of identity is a bit foggy as it is made up of several experiential forms. It is a deception that we have a singular and fixed identity based on forms. Instead, we have a plural identity in the state of flux based on underlying forms. We own the experience of forms by identification with them. For example, someone abuses you, anger rises in you, and you identify with it and become an angry self, by the ownership. And your continuous identification and ownership will make your identity as angry being. You will be convinced, and the world will convince you to make it real for you, though it is deceptive belongingness. The rabbit hole of identity goes very deep, especially because we have learned to live and relate with the world based on made-up identities.

This identity keeps developing in size, strength, and weight, like a snowball effect as we gather experience. It's not a surprise we have preferences for experiences to occur due to associations deposited in our pluralistic identity—a mixture of forms.

As said earlier, human consciousness adopts the limitation, comfort, and discomfort of forms; as a result, the being lives tight and tense due to inner conflicts and divisions of identities adopted. The chronic stress of these identities becomes the suffering of life. Naturally, the being strives to come out of this suffering, but instead of enquiring and responding inwardly at the root level, he/she looks out to retrench, remediate, or replace with outward things, which may help in the short-run but fails to cure at the root level. You can buy a bigger house, a car, change partners, the latest gadget to address the never-ending inner tightness and tension. There is so much appeal for the methods of competition, success, power, violence, and so on; still, there is no respite in the human race.

So, we should try another direction, which is to cure our suffering from where it all started by looking deep inside our being behind our pluralistic identity.

One wonders, there are billions of people walking on earth, how this suffering can be epidemic? And, moreover, why don't we realize our pure consciousness naturally and avoid pluralistic psychological identities? Thus, live with a feeling of joy and fulfillment in life, period.

The reason is a psychological illusion created by identity, which eclipses the awareness to perceive the operation of mental faculties. Naturally, the mind lives in a modification, in which the flow of consciousness is always outward on the objects, and we bypass the consciousness always and almost. Rarely, the awareness settles in a relaxed and undivided state of mind in which one can see how the mind is operating. It is not surprising, people can spend several hours in a movie hall or sports arena, but it is difficult for them to spend thirty minutes to observe themselves calmly. Watching inside yourself—alone and detached becomes very arduous because it is reversing the natural flow of awareness towards its source. Let's understand it through a fictitious example.

Suppose you are born in a big and fully furnished house where the walls, roof, and floor have tiny microscopic bulbs installed in them, so the light is emitted from all sides, and there has never been a power failure. Now, consider, you do everything in it—eat, bathe, sleep, laughing, weeping, and so on, and have never left this home since your birth. What will be your experience of light? You will never realize that there is light existing because there is no source of light in your perception, but only objects are seen as forms in light. Light itself will remain in your blind spot even though everything is seen in its presence. It is a great illusion.

Likewise, in our body-mind framework, our light of consciousness is ever-present in which forms are experienced. But we live ignorant of consciousness and attach to the modified versions of consciousness under the influence of material forms. In this illusion, the *being* tells himself, I am this or that. On the contrary, the ancient sages explained the nature of pure consciousness in simple words: neti-neti, meaning *neither this nor that*.

What should we do? Should we not live in forms? And, is it even practically possible?

The answer lies in cultivating a meditative mind state. Meditation is establishment into pure consciousness where the self is not modified into multiple versions of forms. It is important to know that it does *not* mean, we paralyze us or seclude us from forms to avoid experiences. Instead, this state is devoid of an *illusion* of *identification* with modified consciousness, and only pure consciousness remains in which the experience occurs and is seen as-it-is. It is a state of oneness. A meditative effort is not life-avoiding but a life-affirming experience—identity-less and illusion free. It doesn't require someone to go into the Himalayas. Practically, it's a discipline of tasks undertaken to tune our attention into foundational truth, and reversing the entire cycle of form-based identification. Thus, attaining an attitude of non-identification by establishing into pure consciousness is *wisdom*. And, living with this wisdom is conscious living.

It is not an exaggeration to say that living free of this pluralistic identity is the prime desire of a human being. The feeling of joy is not caused by the existence of *others* but is intrinsic in our innate consciousness. Thus, freedom from versions of self-hood and establishing in pure consciousness brings joy. Freedom is not the ability to do whatever the mind thinks; rather, it is the ability to free up the thinking mind out of modifications in a relaxed and conscious manner. This poem provides a great value to the meditators who are taking their discipline seriously at the experiential level. It depicts that the path of meditation is private, demands courage to question self-hood, and walk into the unknown. The initial phase could be a short struggle due to adjustment with a new way of living—as on the meditative path. The trust in pure consciousness and existence will prove to be the best help. Also, attention directed towards self and reasonably questioning the modification of mind is the best guide to allow a natural discipline to your efforts.

The old analogy given by yogis is still very relevant that pure consciousness is like a vast ocean, and forms are like waves in it. One has to rise above it and sit on a solid rock to watch these forms patiently but remains untouched by them. Finally, surrender oneself into the vast ocean of consciousness, which is the first and final desire of a meditator *being*.

Enjoy reading!

Poem

At the start of the thirtieth year, after my birth, I desired to sketch a ledger of my life. Thus,

I summoned my body, mind, and heart, and solicited, all my retrospective and prospective, desires and outcomes in life.

I looked in the mirror and asked my body, "I enjoy the pride in your companionship. What is your essence?"

I waited long for the answer, hoping for vigor and power, but instead, I heard the weak voice of my body say, "My essence is not more than the food you eat and the way you live with your surroundings."

Is that it? I spoke to myself and sank on the floor.

Thereupon, I reflected on my galvanized mind and asked, "You are the light of my vision and spine of my reason. What do you know of your own, pure and untouched?"

I waited for a long time, in the hope of a grand and gilt echo, but heard the apologetic voice of my mind say, "I am just a blended shadow of the world, which these doors of senses and thought have put upon me. I glue the knowledge to experience to make it explicit for you. I am unknown to anything aboriginal, and all of my reflections are borrowed. I am your organizing closet."

Is that it? I spoke in my mind, and a bubble came up from depression underneath.

Finally, I turned inward to kiss my heart gently and with tender lips of assurance asked, "I know that you fill and filter the blood of love, compassion, desire, fear, temptations, and all emotions to my soul, to make it feel alive and captive in secret ways. What is the unconditional and original in you that lets you do this spiritual osmosis?"

I then waited for a long time, hoping for a melodious rhyme, but heard a regretful resound of my heart say, "I am nothing but a byproduct of the dreams you see or vouch for seeing in your lonely sleep and worldly wakefulness. And I am always obliged by "thought," which helps me to continue my presence. I apologize that you are disillusioned and betrayed by the short-sightedness of my existence."

Hearing this hopelessness, I became omni-lonely, knowing that my body, my mind, and my heart are merely functions empty of any essential meaning life, on which I built my foundations.

Liquidated outwardly, but with an undiluted intention inwardly, I looked around and walked north, toward the ocean through an unconventional detour, determined to know if something inside me was real, originally existential.

Soon, I touched the coastline, and for a moment I stopped, turned back to see the land, and asked myself, "Do you want to leave the known for the love of unknown?"

The answer came from the core of my eclipsed soul—that whatever I got from this land is merely a repressed heart always engaged in unfulfilled self-importance. I didn't have anything to lose anyway.

Thereupon, I looked forward and, knowing the meaninglessness of known and feeling the curiosity for the unknown; I entered the ocean fearlessly.

Without looking back, I walked hastily, and let the white waves wash off the dirt of land from my face.

As I moved on, false confidence gripped me; that all the previous versions of myself were washed away, and I became a new self.

I would have walked miles evaluating myself like this until I fell off the hidden cliff inside the ocean.

There was no ground and gravity to aid assured walking on my legs of the past and future. And, surrender was the way to go.

At that moment, all pretense evaporated like a mist, as if my body, my mind, and my heart had been just reborn to learn how to coordinate in the state of "now."

I closed my eyes and left myself to the waves and learned how to "let go," which I enjoyed for some time.

Later, I touched upon a small rock standing upright in the center of the rumbling ocean.

I pulled myself up to sit on it and looked around the pure, endless ocean—its waves on the blue surface and uprising splashes—and a downward-looking silent, clear sky.

For a very long time, I gazed at the ocean around and lost my sense of proprioception. Am I moving, or cosmos is moving around me? Or are we moving together in unison?

A faint curiosity crept within me for a definition, location, and time, but instead, I closed my tired eyes, and let go of the charm of knowing anything, anymore.

A strange satisfaction arose in me. I was in the state of pure knowing, without the knot of knower and known.

Upon waking, I realized that, for the very first time, my mirror, reflections, and dreams were not with me, and I sat up in a meditative posture to see the circling ocean around me was dancing with no rhyme or reason.

In the dancing ocean, there was no mirror to view my "self." It saved me from making any definition.

Without a mirror, I conceived that there are no forms, and the formless is a form against all the forms that the mind perceives. Holding to a concept of formlessness is in no way better than forms unless the conception itself is broken.

Upon breaking the mirror, I was left to reflect and liberate myself from definitions.

However, the glue of my mind was still working to experience the waves and to discover the new laws, hidden in them.

When the waves rose and died down in many degrees of movement, it made me realize that life and death are neither against each other nor sequential, but they are together all the time, and one cannot exist without the other.

In a moment, one wave created thousands of waves, and other times thousands of waves folded into one. Likewise, life is a transmutation of energy from one to many and from many to one. Therefore, life continues, and there is no permanent death.

The ocean remains gapless despite all the turbulence and crashing of waves. Thus, the law of oneness was realized in my heart and lit a true lamp of compassion.

No wave exists in isolation; it rises with the force of previous waves and ends with a push for the next one, explained the cause and effect in existence. All laws themselves are respective and relative to the levels of existence.

In the company of the ocean, my mind perceived and washed away all realizations like the waves wash one another. Thus, the glue which grips my experiences, loosened. Thereupon, the content of consciousness was emptied.

Dreams became meaningless as my heart forgot to move in a direction, as waves changed their courses for the love of others.

Days and nights passed in this loneliness, and my body, my mind, and my heart worked naturally in unison and forgot the mirror, reflections, and dreams.

One day during the early dawn, when the sky was modestly red with the warm love of the morning star, the blue ocean started whirling fast around the rock and rose up to greet the heavenly abode.

I stood upon the rock on its hood to see that the ocean was rising everywhere in the perimeter of my outbound vision.

At that very moment, a soundless but centripetal voice came from all directions and asked me, "O meditator, what is your final wish?"

My soul moved up and down the ladder of consciousness, from unconscious to subconscious to conscious to superconscious levels, and stepped on to the final rung to reach home.

But soon, I realized that there wasn't any wish left for me to rest in the home of any existential realm. And, I must be homeless before I make this existence, my home. So, I let go this ladder of levels, to live as-it-is.

Then the last spark of curiosity to know the ocean twinkled, but surprisingly, my soul washed away that final curiosity.

I remained silent and looked at myself to see the greatest miracle— that at the center of the whirling ocean, this soul is nothing but water sparks of the ocean continually moving in and out of it.

And that was the last realization that the existence is omni-flush.

The moving ocean rose up to the sun, and with a thunderclap, it fell back on the rock, and nothingness prevailed.

In this profound silence, it appeared that now the ocean longs for the emptiness of the rock to be filled again.

Strangely, the wisdom waits for the wise more than the wise longs for the wisdom, and only the oceanic wish prevails; human desires are just human.

O beloved meditator, as said by the wisest among men, Gautam the Buddha,

"Gate, gate, paragate, parasamgate, bodhi swaha!
Gone, gone, far gone, forever gone, and be consumed in the light."
So be it.

Silence Occurs

Sounds are produced in silence. Sounds are consumed in silence.
Silence is the backdrop of all sounds.

Prelude

"Everything in life is vibration"
– Albert Einstein

We live in a sea of sounds spread in space, and it is not an overemphasis to say that we are the creatures of sound as well. Our physical and mental activities—speech, thoughts, feelings, and emotions are expressions of sound energy. Moreover, at a very subtle level beneath physical and mental levels when we meditate on our being, it is still a calm sea of sound energy, which can be called the sound of silence.

Perhaps this is the reason that sounds affect us at all ages. A sweet lullaby puts a newborn to sleep, a siren creates chills of fear in grown- ups, and a meaningful song can help cope up, with the pain of old age disease or maybe death.

This is a great insight because types of vibrations can be cause and remedy for ease or disease in our physical and mental bodies. Thus, it is immensely important to understand our relationship with sound and silence.

Have you seen a wooden plank in the ocean moving towards the coastline? Actually, the plank never moves, but it gets handed over from one wave to another and just appears to be moving. Likewise, sound travels through a medium when the energy moves by vibrating the particles and appears sound is moving. Obviously, the quality of sound perceived is based on the medium. What does it mean for us in terms of sounds perceived from the outer world and of our own inner being?

In the outer world, sounds are created by striking at least two objects together, and we perceive them through comparison and contrast; and   are conditioned by their persistence. We classify them, identify with their sources, and like or dislike them. As we are psychological beings, we create a judgmental attitude. It is true for our social relationships as well.

For the inner world, it is not about likes, dislikes, or judgmental attitude, but knowing the sound of our being is important. Every moment we feel sensations in body and mind as vibrations, and if we keep observing and moving deep inwardly, we will observe an exceptionally calm, non-instrumental humming. Probably, it is our original sound. Let's call it—*Sound of being*. What is the source of this non-instrumental basic sound? And, this *sound of being* is heard against what background? Let's call it *Silence*.

To draw a parallel, it is worth observing the sound of a simple bell ringing, sustaining as a reverberation before dying out slowly. Tune into the silence before, the silence after, and the underlying silence on which sound is traveling.

In the same way, it is worth to observe our own *Sound of being* originating out of *Silence* as its background. Find a relatively quiet place, neither soundproof nor public place. Sit in a relaxed posture and do a survey of your body head to toe to find any tightness and relax a little bit more. Visualize yourself as ears only, situated in the center of the world, a sea of sounds. Tune yourself to the farthest sound coming towards you. Examine one by one by moving your attention circularly around your body, and each time, receive it coming radially inward. Attend to the sounds and the gap for some time.

In this way, start with the outer world of sounds and turn inwardly by comparing and leaving behind extraneously received sounds, one after another.

First, examine the physical body, head to toe to perceive any sound, like breath moving between navel and throat, or pulse, or any other form. The key is to be absorbed fully into the experience of your body and its sounds. Attend to the sounds and the gap for some time.

Thereupon, examine the mental body in terms of your thinking voice, emotions, and feelings, which are spoken inside. Note if any song or voice is coming from sub-conscious. Listen to your internal sounds carefully without making any meaning out of it. Attend to the sounds and the gap for some time.

Thereupon, examine your inner aliveness into your sense of being, feeling of presence. Do not create or force concentration on anything; instead, let go off your focus on anything and stay to the feeling of beingness. No manipulation or creativity is needed. If some physical or mental sounds are coming, it's OK, do not push them away or get caught up with them. Stay with the sense of being as it is. There is no turbulence possible with this sense. It is impersonal You beneath your personality. At this stage, only two things are important— Sense of beingness and receptivity. With these two in a pure state, a non-instrumental humming is felt. You can call it Sound of being. Do not imagine or try to develop anything to experience it. If you develop it in one way, it will be destroyed by the other way. If you try to keep it, it will be lost in your trial. Do not hold; else it will go away. Just be your natural being and be receptive. Let it be a natural and automatic flow of humming and rest in its peace.

You will find this *Sound of being* is always present but gets avoided due to the noise around.

Can you further examine from where it is coming? Is pure Silence in its background?

This short poem elaborates on the nature of Silence.

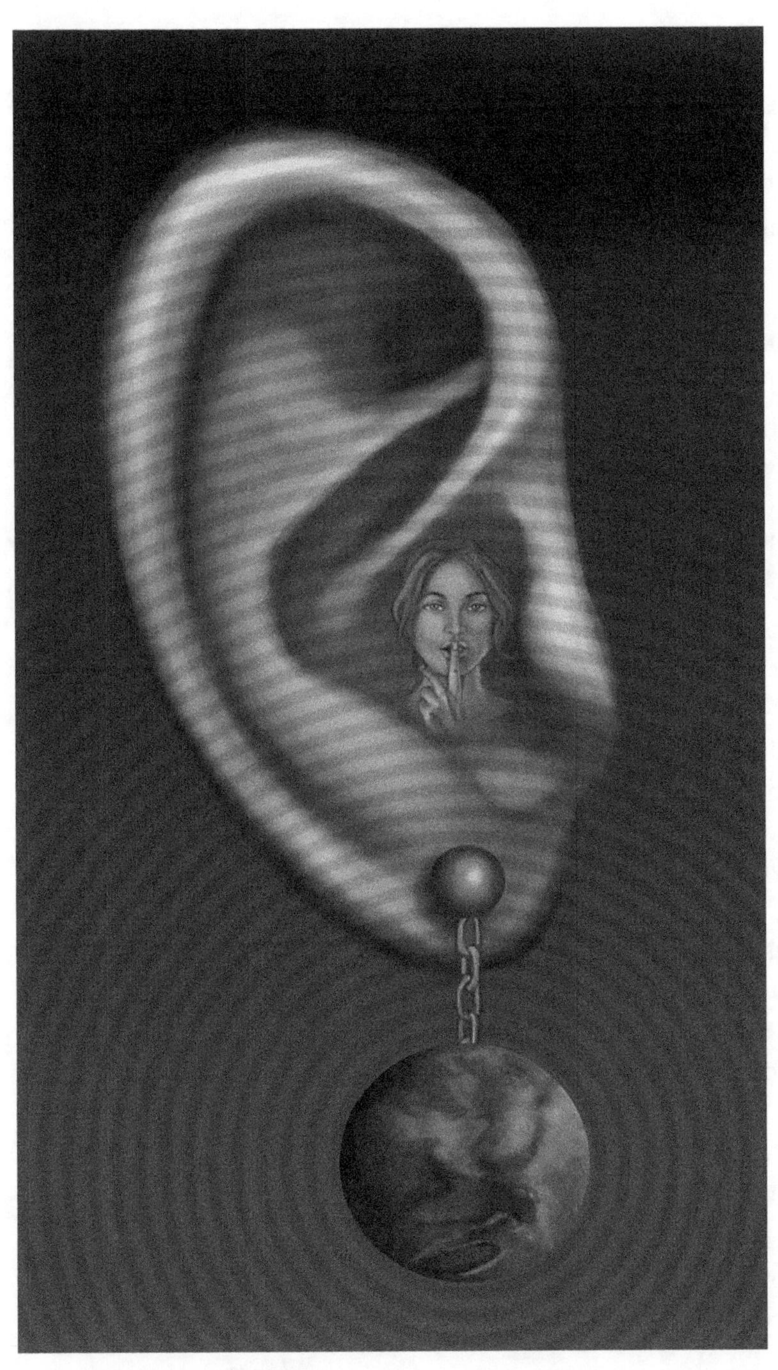

Poem

O Beloved,
Can you clap and create a sound?
And can you clap louder and create another sound?
Congratulations! You can graduate and multiply sounds,
and make it many and mightier than the previous rounds.

Now, can you un-clap and create *Silence*?
And can you un-clap harder and create stronger *Silence*?
Sadho! Sadho!
Now, you know the science of *Silence.*

Truly, sounds occur, and *Silence* "is."
But, sadly, we assume the opposite.
Consequently, in this world of sounds,
chasing after *Silence* looks so profound.

And, we search for it in the mountains or in caves,
follow gurus, seek knowledge, or sit near the mute graves.
Still, we miss its fountainhead,
flowing just beneath our *being's* bed.

Thus, for a sound-addicted mind,
let us begin with its opposite,
and anyhow, as one must start where he is.
Who knows by the end he loses all, he assumed was "his?"

So, let us begin within,
with the means of sounds, we confer,
and seek what lies beneath them.
Which makes the Silence to occur?

O Beloved, in its purest form,
   Silence occurs...
         when the mute gap eats
         the borders of mind,
         to subsist itself continuously,
         where thinking is born of it, and not designed.
   Silence occurs...
         When the *being* walks on a sign-less path,
         unguarded by the past and future.
         It remains deeply relaxed and receptive,
         and senses a serene silence behind all of its fore features.
   Silence occurs...
         When the stillness sings
         without the burden of sound.
         Where primal rhythm remains,
         without any cause of "two," to pound.
   Silence occurs...
         When the drop falls
         through the layers of air,
         and merges in the ocean,
         and cares no more to find itself anywhere.
   Silence occurs...
         When the *being* stands before the existence
         as one mirror before another.
         The law of exchange is baffled
         when one offers the "void" to others.
   Silence occurs...
         When the death
         is transcended by life
         and self knows both are born of each other,
         and this knowledge makes your inner-self wise.

Silence occurs...
    Where the center of the body
    meets the center of heart,
    meets the center of the mind.
    Thereupon, you lose this center in a nameless bind.
Silence occurs...
    When the sensors open out,
    but its sense opens in,
    and the self knows this body is merely a medium
    to experience the livingness of the *being*.
Silence occurs...
    When mechanics of life
    transform into the magic of life,
    and the freshness prevails.
    Your *being* wonders! And it remains no more stale.

O Beloved, may thee enter the silence like a humming wind through the window of spirit and conceive a song to sing forever.

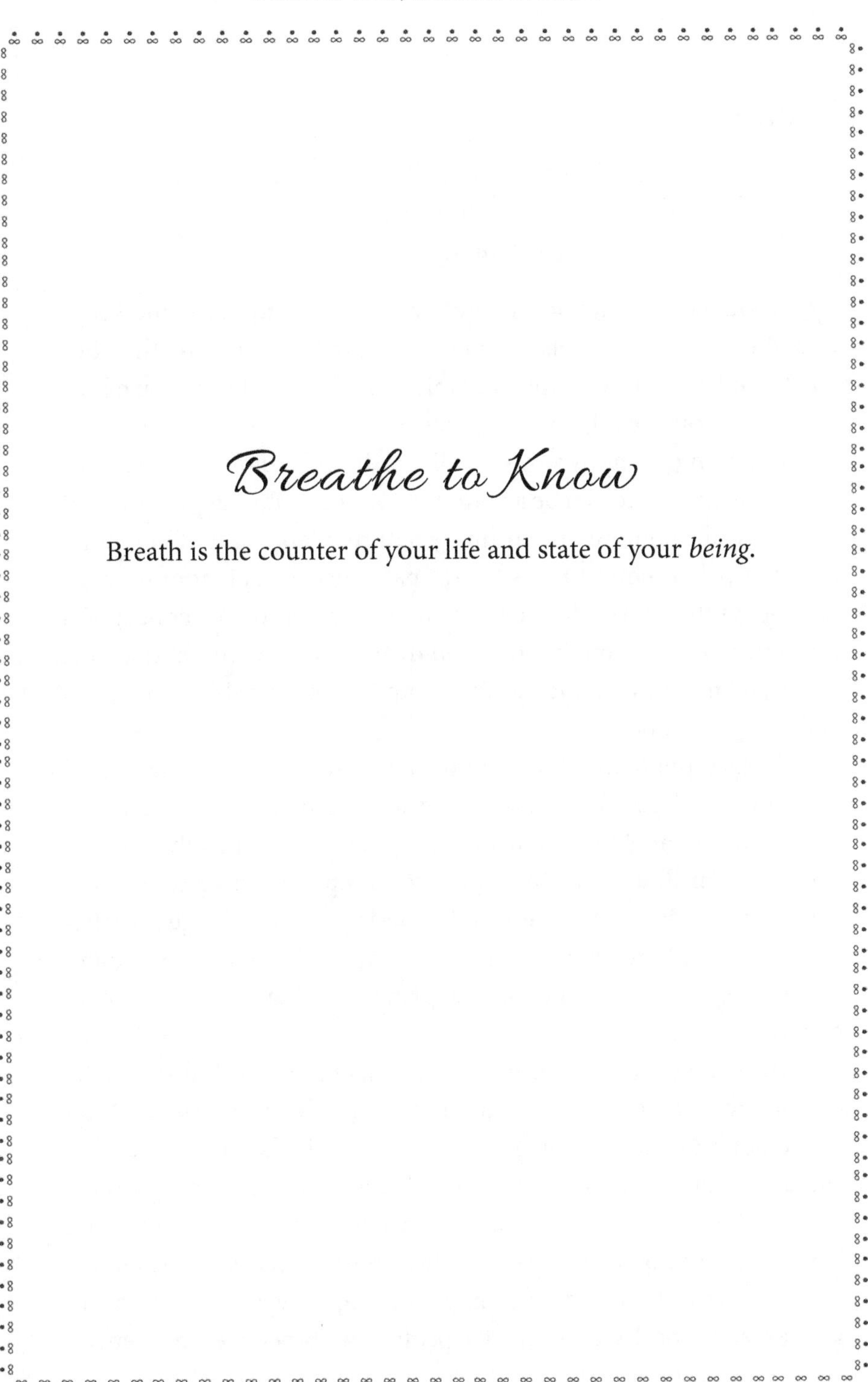

Breathe to Know

Breath is the counter of your life and state of your *being*.

Prelude

One who understands the breath quickly
tastes the ecstasy of liberation.
— Gorakhshastra

A good handyman knows how to organize his toolbox, and keeps the most usable tools accessible. Nature has given breath as our most usable and useful tool, available to all. We all should learn how to use it for our health and happiness.

Breathing is synonymous with living. It is a fundamental and most obvious activity and can be a voluntary or non-voluntary action. But due to its autonomous and ordinary nature, a large part of humanity does not pay attention to its functions, hence, lives ignorant of the knowledge that can be derived from it. It is a common misconception that only monks and meditators should learn its various functions. Due to this, many of us do not enquire about its innumerable, direct, and definitive benefits.

A large population gets comfortable merely by its theoretical education and gets concerned only in case of health issues. It is important to know that using breathing function rightfully not only save us from illness but takes us to deep, meaningful mental states in meditation. Direct and experiential knowledge enriches our *being,* and breath can be a very handy medium. It is a firsthand experience, not a secondhand explanation that brings value to our lives.

Mostly, we all know, breathing and its pattern is influenced by our physical energy, mental state, and levels of consciousness. What we do not know commonly is that the reverse is also true. Breathing can also counter influence these processes, if disciplined rightfully. Due to this two-way relation, human beings can derive immense benefits by tuning into the rightful breathing patterns. For example, coherent and rhythmic breathing can help prepare this body to gain excellent health and can give profound immersive experiences.

Specifically, for meditators, the breath can bring sharpness in their meditative efforts.

This poem has two sections. Part-A elaborates the glory of breath, and Part-B provides twenty-one breath meditations. These are convenient means to move inwardly, and convenience depends upon the specific person's attitude. Therefore, the given practices are sort of a recommendation only, instead of a mandatory course. So, apply them with a comfortable and curious mindset; and if you have the curiosity to know all, then all can be worked upon. Be cautious of one rule: take one meditation at a time for a few days/weeks to understand its depth.

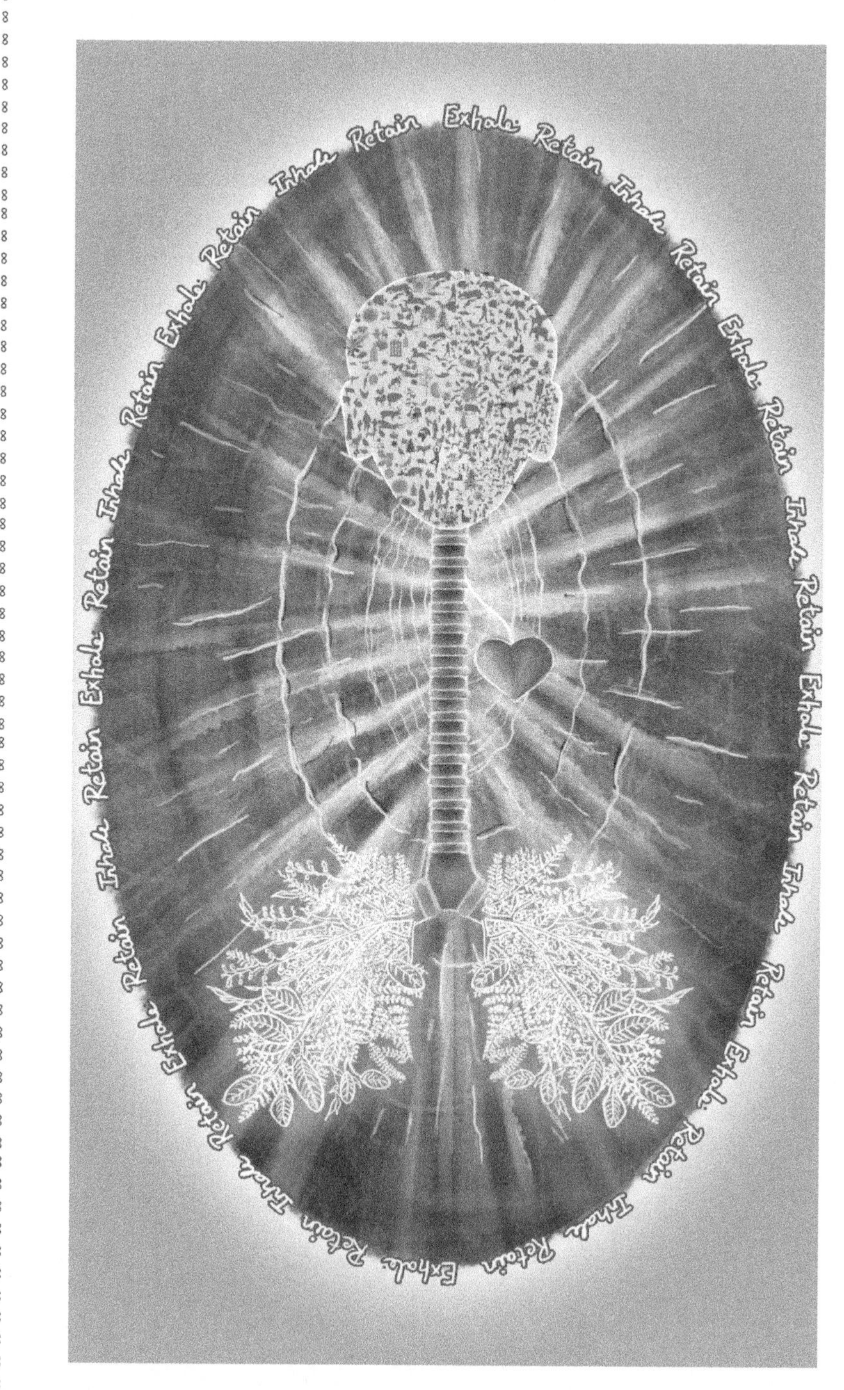

Exhale Retain Inhale Retain Exhale Retain Inhale Retain Exhale Retain Inhale Retain Exhale Retain Inhale Retain Exhale Retain Inhale Retain Exhale Retain Inhale Retain Exhale Retain Inhale

Poem

O Beloved,
you have the keys to the cosmic treasure,
available within you without measure.
Doesn't matter, rich or poor, weak or strong,
a pundit or dimwit, short or long.

Impossible to lose this key as it belongs to you.
In all moods and modes, it keeps you to continue,
from the moment of your birth, till your death,
the only faithful companion is your lovely breath.

Breath is a recurring assertion of your existence.
A boundary between life and death, but it's a delicate fence.
For the mindless, it is an activity without much sense.
But for the mindful, it is a gifted door to the immense.

Breath is like a moving wave, on an energy string,
having a network in all modalities and bodies of your *being*.
Influences the unobvious inside with an obvious side of the string,
and the opposite is also true if you can sense its rhythm and ping.

Through the chimney of nostril's dyad,
the *being* vents out the smoke, simmering inside,
changes the wavelength and frequency of breath and its flight.
But, when watched mindfully, opens possibilities to access the insight.

The mindful catches this intuitive knowledge,
to connect inside and uses the breath as a bridge.
This connection enables it, as a controlling junction,
which makes it a valuable utility for transformative function.

The breath has three simple sections:
inhalation, exhalation, and retention
which demonstrates the petite prototype of a larger life,
similar to your birth, death, and resurrection.

Knowing the beats of the breath,
and its rise and its depth.
You cultivate its awareness as a bridge to beyond,
and probe the secrets of another side, to correspond.

Keep following your breath as a guide,
Witness its form and then the hidden force inside,
Know how it reacts to your inner world, one by one.
You will trust this process more than anything else ever done.

It's the success story of the most basic thing in life, available
ordinary. Over the fancy glory of material things in life, earned
extraordinarily. One who knows its pith and play,
knows the DNA of his or her cast and clay.

O Beloved,
your simple breath which moves to and fro,
do not waste it, thinking it as a mindless flow.
It is a magical pump of your inner stove to glow.
Just be mindful of the breath and breathe to know.

Be easy but esoteric,
and enjoy its ride and flow.
Just remember to be aware,
with focus, and breathe to know, and breathe to know.

Twenty-one Breath Meditations

The following cues can be used to meditate using breath:

1. On knowledge of breath's relationship to body and mind:
   Watch the movement of breath when you have a relaxed mind.
   Watch the movement of breath when you have a stressed mind.
   Be very attentive, as breath is a very sensitive rope, hooked in all functions of your body and mind.

2. On knowledge of earth element:
   Watch the incoming breath as a solid, heavy stroke.
   Watch the outgoing breath like a soft, cotton-like smoke.
   When breath seeds "vitality" inside, life grows out.
   Feel the earth in it, which keeps you stable and stout.

3. On knowledge of water element:
   Watch the incoming breath as humid mist moving upstream.
   Watch the outgoing breath as a warm channel moving downstream.
   For the mindful it has a head, body, and tail, flowing up and down,
   furnishing the nature of fluidity, by feeling this flow around.

4. On knowledge of fire element:
   As you see, the fire wins over the gravity of earth,
   watch the fire of your exhaling outward breath.
   It wins over the gravity of holding the breath inside,
   this makes the breath relaxed, light, and easy to glide.
   As the fire annihilates impurities
   and make things pure and glow,
   watch the outgoing breath annihilating defilements,
   to purify the mind, and let it glow.

5. On knowledge of air:

> Watch the circulation of air,
>
> and its action as weightless drier,
>
> evaporating the moisture,
>
> living as a medium without any posture.

6. On knowledge of sound:

> While breathing slow, watch the endpoints of retention.
>
> Increase the length of these gaps slowly in succession.
>
> Thereupon, in vast stillness, know you are only a "presence."
>
> In this way, sustain attention to listen to the sound of silence.
>
> Knowing that all formulated sounds are mere modalities
>
> of a silently humming ocean, where waves are abnormalities.
>
> The knower of this knows the nature of primal vibrations. The sounds around us are spikes out of their formal actions. (**Read poem:** *Silence occurs* to know more on it)

7. On the perception of forms:

> When breathing out, know its farthest-reaching point.
>
> When breathing in, know its deepest dissolving point.
>
> Perceive its form, resolving and dissolving, in and outside. Perceive these two nodes, as if connected via a hollow pipe.
>
> Cognition and recognition create a form and shape of breath.
>
> Feel the force of sensation, creating its rise and depth.
>
> Likewise, examine all external and internal forms in mind. The world you see is nothing but the sum total of forms defined.

8. On the sensation of touch:
   When the inflow of breath strikes against nostril walls,
   it creates pressure in hollowness and sensations in halls.
   This sensation creates knowledge of your limit and location,
   then the knowledge becomes a thought as a tool of separation.

9. On physics of life-breath:
   Upon inhalation, when the bags of lungs expand,
   and increase in volume,
   the pressure in the ribcage decreases,
   and creates a bigger room.
   Physical laws act automatically to create equilibrium,
   thus exhalation happens through the muscular medium.
   In this way, action and inaction are synchronized,
   obeying the basic laws of physics in every breath of life.

   Your life does not like "greed" to store.
   Nor does it allow the freedom to exhale more.
   No one has a passport to win over it and proclaim,
   life is easy in surrendering to the rules of this game.

   While breathing, mindfulness of your will and natural force
   brings an astute sense of instrumentation about your life course.
   You realize existence is working to support "me" at every moment,
   and this creates in you an attitude of connection,
    otherwise dormant.

10. On knowledge of inner organs:
    Look within with closed eyes;
    listen within with inner ears,
    at the movements inside,
    when the breath changes gears.

Feel the moving breath as blood in the moving spot;
examine the interdependent moving parts and
their knots.
Synchronize organs and breathe in regular, rhythmic
moments.
Remain persistent and alert to feel these movements.
How the ribcage expands
and muscles contract.
How the autonomic system passes,
the control to your "will" to act.

Part by part observation of the vertebrae and staff of spine,
brings new wisdom about your rigid view of self and
"mine."
How the throat, heart, lungs, abdomen, and torso behave
brings knowledge of energy centers in the hidden caves.

11. On knowledge of management of mind:
Breath is the best guide of mind and its elements.
Therefore, befriend your breath and watch its sentiments.
No matter how tedious initially it may be "to be
synchronized" in the present,
in the end, it's a meaningful tool for your mind
management.

There is no bigger gift,
than the gift of now,
Truly, you will wonder yourself,
and it will make you wow!

For negative perceptions, thoughts,
emotions and feelings,
your breath can be used
to discipline and for healing.

12. On knowledge of clean consciousness free from thoughts:
   When the unwanted thoughts agitate the mind and build up a gloom,
   be mindful of pure breath coming in and going out,
   and use it like a broom.

   Watch your breathing and stop in between,
   when your mind is mixed with thoughts.
   Now, watch your stop and breathe in between,
   and see your mind is pure and without dots.

   For the attentive, it's a magic wand,
   to check and cease any hidden knots.
   When the purity of breath accompanies the awareness,
   your mind is free of compulsion and enjoys the bareness.

13. On the purity of consciousness free from extreme feelings:
   Watch your breath
   when your body shivers with excessive emotions.
   Watch your breath
   when your body is free of any undue motion.

   For the attentive,
   it's a handy medicine
   to prevent any future regrets,
   due to a painful explosion.

14. On the action of the will before it is triggered:
   Watch,
   when your breath is willfully geared.
   Watch,
   when your breath is a volunteer.

   For the attentive,
   it's a sieve
   to filter the seen
   from the seer.

15. On overcoming stress and anxiety—
When you feel life situations have left you in gloom,
and you are shut in a dark and doorless room,
notice that the sync between breath and mind is shoddy.
Attain a fixed posture, relax your breath, and tune it
with your mental body.

If you feel rigidity and pain anywhere,
breathe your slow but deep vibrations into that sphere.
Voluntary breathing can be used to gain sobriety.
Move slowly to non-voluntary function to come out
of anxiety.

16. On breath as a body of vital energy/prana—
Breath is an outer vessel, and prana is its soul.
Prana energizes life to rock and roll.
Due to the movement of breath, the pranas are sown.
In the retention of breath, the essence of pranas is known.

While inhaling,
be aware of the quality of your vital energy.
While retaining internally,
be aware of the quality of your vital energy.

While exhaling,
be aware of the quality of your vital energy.
While retaining externally,
be aware of the quality of your vital energy.

These are the four switches
of your pranic abode.
Flipping them correctly will
activate your vitality chord.

17. On rhythm between dynamic and static forces:
Watch silence before a relaxed inhalation up-surging
from it.

Watch silence after a relaxed exhalation sub-merging in it.
Watch silence as a turning point in between.

Watch this as a wavelet spun out of two silent nodes
and dying back in [them].

Know that dynamic and static forces
are two sides of the same coin.
Thus, discipline both using breath,
and witness the point of their joint.

18. On the togetherness of arising and dying events:
Existence is gapless, and no one exists alone.
Things arise together and live in others when they are gone.
Breath exhibits this belongingness in all cyclic stations—
inhalation and exhalation and inner and outer retentions.

When one dies out, it gives space for others to appear.
They live as law without any love or fear.
Watch their action together and one by one.
Know the doer while doing it and how it is done.

19. On involuntary action and relation to the formless:
Breathe in and know its origin as directionless.
Breathe out and know its origin as directionless.
Thus, while breathing in and out, know its origin as
directionless.

Now, observe behind the two origins, to know the
urge to breathe, as directionless.
This urge springs out of the non-voluntary physical
movement.
Look earnestly, this autonomous momentum and its
midpoint.

Be very slowly established in this non-voluntary
awareness. Leave clasps of oscillation out, and float
into the formless.

Witness earnestly, its non-voluntary movement,
until it flows without "will," empty of its development.

May you encounter repressed images as you relax
and unwind,
just surpass these images bubbling up from the floor
of the mind.

20. On self-perception meditation:
Merge your very slow, deep, and rhythmic breathing
with awareness and sound of silence in your *being*.
Practice these three together to synchronize.
It becomes a deeply relaxing and revealing exercise.

Slowly, the perception becomes subtle and refined.
It will make your *being* feel meaningful and aligned.
It is an utterly magical meditation;
It can be done anytime and at any location.

21. On awareness meditation—
With easy and pure attention,
watch your natural breath per lap continually.
Be aware of feeling the rare inner joy of its coming
and going,
and flowing through your entire body map.
Retain the equipoise,
about this extremely relaxed weather, created inside.
Retain this rhythmic flow,
as it releases the repressed and rigid knots situated
inside. It's like bathing with the warm water of
awareness,
and a bar of soap, as breath.
Keep the water running,
and wash your length and breadth.

Now, put the soap away to bathe in awareness,

and let go of any froth remaining.
When the form of breath is broken,
awareness knows the subtleties without naming.

Your breath is a proven cause,
of immense joy, calmness, and wisdom.
It only appears to be a hook of life,
and bondage but truly is a tool of freedom.

Sync up with your breath deeply,
and meditate.
Don't waste life in the sink of senses.
Look inside and elevate.

O Beloved,
there would be one last breath in life,
after which it stops to flow.
Before that comes, turn inside,
and breathe to know, and breathe to know.

Shunyasati, the Mindful Tea Maker

Mindful activity is aligning your action
and awareness with activity.

Prelude

*The mind is the forerunner of all mental objects. Suffering follows
an impure mind as the cart follows the footsteps of the Ox.*
—Dhammapada, Verse 1

What is the mind? And what is mindfulness?

Our desires, thoughts, actions, and experiences shape our mind. This shape gets solidified by continuous engagement, habits, and conditioning. Thus, our life is designed by the solid shape of the mind, we carry around. It's our choice how we want to cultivate our mind. Either we can let this solid shape to control us heedlessly, and cause suffering, or we can cultivate the right mental factors to create a happy life.

Before we attempt to choose anything, we need to understand the fundamental nature of experience which is not manipulated, desired, or created but realized *as it is, as it happens*. The awareness of this quality of experience is called *mindfulness*. It can be learned, practiced, and cultivated over time, as a meditative process.

To sum up, one can say mindfulness meditation is to cultivate a quality of awareness about the occurrence of experience in its entirety, including the experiencer. How to do it?

Cultivating mindfulness is like gardening, and the meditator is like a gardener. To grow a tree and reap fruits you need healthy seed, fertile land, the right care, necessary protection, and patience to let it grow and bear fruits. In practical terms, four things are essential, as following: Intention, Attitude, Activity, and Receptivity.

The *solid intention* is your healthy seed, but the drive should be intrinsic, independent, and primary. It is important for two reasons.

Firstly, if meditation is due to a borrowed condition, let's say due to group pressure, then it will fail to produce results if the condition is not met at any moment. For example, hot water is used for cooking, but if the stove is off, water cannot cook because heat is not its intrinsic property. Similarly, if the drive is not intrinsic sooner or later, you will leave the effort. Many people are not able to continue meditation because they never based it on their inner drive, but because of some other external motives.

Secondly, if meditation is due to dependent or a secondary value, then it will fail once the secondary value is attained. For example, many believe yoga is for body toning, or Yoga Nidra is for relaxation. The moment these benefits are derived, the effort is lost to go deep into it.

An intrinsic intention makes it more seductive than a serious task.

The right attitude is your fertile land. As said in Amritbindu Upanishad, Verse 2— "Mana eva manushyanam karanam bandha mokshayoho." It means, "A man is as good as his mind (attitude); Bondage or liberation are in your mind."

As the water follows gravity, our actions follow attitude. Our way of living is dependent upon our attitude—physical and mental both. We react to a situation based on the attitude we carry. And, the settlement of attitude in us is a mixture of perceptions, emotions, feelings, beliefs, values, associations, and ego identity, accumulated over time.

A sincere meditator knows the importance of realizing the attitude and cultivating the right attitude. This is most helpful in advancing the chosen practice.

To see its magic, let's say you are working on mindfulness meditation techniques, and build an attitude of *mindfulness* in your meditation practice. Then this attitude will shape up everything in its direction. How?

Normally you breathe but add mindful attitude to breathe mindfully.

Normally you eat but add mindful attitude to eat mindfully.

Normally you walk but add mindful attitude to walk mindfully.

Normally you talk but add mindful attitude to talk mindfully.

Normally you think but add mindful attitude to think mindfully.

And so on.

A similar thing will happen if you take the attitude of simplicity or spontaneity, and so on, based on your practice. *The right attitude* will allow your intention to grow healthy in the intended direction. Therefore, having the *right attitude* is key for meditation.

The right activity is like nurturing to develop. It is acquiring the right knowledge, choosing the right set of tools and techniques, and applying them with focus and determination.

One wonder, how to know what is the *right activity* required for me? It depends upon you, remember it's your show, so you have to decide to step forward, what type of shoe you need depends upon your foot size, and road conditions you are walking on. It can be practicing alone or in a group or both. (Note: A simple mindfulness technique   is explained in the last section of this book for reference).

Lastly, a meditator is required to be patiently *Receptive*. Attitude and activity are outer qualities, whereas receptivity is the intrinsic key quality, for awareness. Attitude and activity show how one reacts, and receptivity is a quality that shows how one grasps.

With this basic framework, the gardener style meditator cultivates mindfulness and reaps the countless benefits. What are some of the key benefits?

Mindfulness changes the idea of self and the way we see ourselves and the world around us. Our viewpoints shift from a mute consumer of life-events thrown at us, to an insightful witness by directly perceiving the truth of experience. We attain wisdom about the nature of things as they really are. It trains the mind to see the truth in the present moment and saves the meditator from getting caught up in worries about the future and regrets of the past. Also, it provides a systematic way to survey our mental factors in the field of awareness, either at a surface level or deep within the mind. Finally, it loosens up the idea of solidity of body-mind construct and lets the suffering evaporate, and the *being* lives liberated and happy.

This chapter provides an in-depth perspective on mindfulness in action. It elaborates on the importance of *intention, activity, attitude, and receptivity* for mindfulness meditation. Further, it explains mindfulness, by classifying experience of activity into *what, why, when, who, and how.* To make it simple, tea-making activity is chosen to describe how one can be mindful while preparing it.

Read it mindfully to enjoy it fully.

Poem

"OBeloved, this is a call for all men and women, sitting in the houses or walking out in the sun. Now is the time to liberate yourself and live free; come out! And be my guest for a mindful cup of tea," shouted Shunyasati, the mindful tea maker.

On that morning, when the sun was still hiking up behind the mountains, to hop over the clouds for its resurrection, the call of the tea maker in the village was an exotic song, but also an interruption.

On the other side of the mountain, the villagers were still getting ready to welcome the daystar, and make up their day lists, when the tea maker walked in, as a hypnotic hawker out of the mist.

His magnetic appeal pushed some villagers out of their routines; they circled around the tea maker and packed up their daily lists as if they were no more the order takers.

"What do you have *got* to offer us this morning?" asked one of them.

Shunyasati remained involved in the tea making, and without turning up his head, he said, "I bring you magic in a mindful cup of tea, along with the deep philosophy, science, and art of its recipe.

"Rare are those who know it, fortunate are those who grow it, and blessed are those who glow with it.

"This is an art of knowing the bare truth without deformation and science of direct realization of the self and its transformation.

"In the mindfulness of each passing moment, the *being* functions with ease and accepts its fruit as it is.

"One attains a compassionate heart for all without any split and wisdom about the functions of his or her mind distinctly, bit by bit.

"Quality of experience is fresh and worry-free, and freedom from your compulsive reactions brings you clarity."

"O Shunyasati, strong is your offer but not stronger than the demands of the day, which have already shrunk our time to pursue our play."

"We could pay you today for whatever you made for yourself in the stock; this way, we both will be happy and be done in favor of clock," said the villagers, laughingly and urged agility.

Replied the tea maker, "O Beloved, I would have made it for all those who live oblivious, blind, but busy; unfortunately, this is rightfully neither possible nor easy.

"No one else can compose for you or impose it on you, including yourself. Rather, nurture it patiently, and let it cultivate in its natural health.

"As every sleepwalker and dream weaver must open his or her own eyes to awake, and nobody else can wake up for them, for goodness sake. "Wisdom of mindfulness cannot be given or granted or exchanged with any other thing to thee. It is to be worked upon to be deserved, and none could have it entitled, as free.

"Albeit, the recipe can be shared to begin the play, but truly, you must find it, grind it yourself, and end it in your own way. So, tell me, are you determined to learn and earn it today?"

Upon hearing this, many villagers left the tea maker, but a few remained and were laughed at by those who were the bid breakers.

One of the villagers, while walking out, asked in a frenzy, "O tea brewer, what made you so arrogant to call upon us as sleepwalkers and dream weavers? What are we missing in life without this mindfulness?" Said Shunyasati, the mindful tea maker, "O Beloved, it's not insolence but a rooster's morning peep that falls upon as a disturbance on the ears of those who are addicted to the sleep.

"Countless are the reasons to be mindful, but let us begin with few for beginners, that is rightful.

"In this world, when life becomes a reckless whirl of desires, it sucks the spirit in mess of cravings, swirling around, like helpless, hanging ears who are forced to attend any passing sound.

"And your *being* becomes a living newspaper, whose knowledge of self is informational and shaped by social scrapers.

"This newspaper life is busy in making up a personality of its own, by flashing the favorites on the front page and pushing the dislikes to the back-page filler zone.

"The news changes daily, but the theme remains the same; likewise, the mind modifies daily, barring the rules of the game.

"The patterns and habits give a face to the mind, which uses expressions of names and forms for itself to bind.

"You believe in free will; still, you seek bonding and suffer its bondage; this happens only when your mindfulness is out of range.

"In this way, life appears to be busy from its head to tail, but the quality of your experience remains the same: static and stale.

"You remain engaged in the older versions of yourself and overlook the 'new' born out of the old self.

"A gap is created between what you think you are and what you truly are. With this gap, when you live in a world of expectations, your measurement of effort and aim is always a fiction.

"This constant gap between your static self-image and dynamic reality as it is, is stretched by self-denial, which gives space to random desires to self-please.

"These two active keys of denial and desire wind up the *being* and create deception and delusion of ego inside, as a solid thing.

"For this unhappy, stiff ego, whatever you have, will never be enough, and with this attitude, finding peace within yourself will be very tough.

"Thereupon, your agitated mind becomes a dark room cluttered with mental objects, and you fall down and fail by them, again and again as a blind subject.

"The fear of falling becomes a natural tendency, which blurs your reasoning and clarity to foresee.

"Thereupon, the fear-driven alertness takes a popular position, and you always battle, either to escape life or to push away others, in fear of collision.

"With the lamp of mindfulness, the *being* is like a gleaming flyover, who witnesses the passing traffic, either in a jam or loosely crossing over.

"O Beloved, in this world of words, our knowledge is symbolic and secondhand, and instead of living by ourselves, we live as herds.

"Suppose the world is a big library and you are a book, do you ever wonder about your existence, originality, and *real* look?

"What you know about your life is kind of credit history of popular ideas and images, which makes your book of life, in which events are in the index, and your reactions detailed out in pages.

"So, your life book is a story of a rigid self, looks for identification and belongingness in the classified genres arranged in various shelves, which are pre-defined in the blocks of library. But, you know. The truth flows unclassified, like a wild river, which is quite contrary.

"Thereby, we miss the vastness of our existence and the changing moments of the reality of our lives and its experience.

"Conversely, mindfulness makes us available to access unbiased cognition, by enabling us to witness the makeup of this self-ideation.

"Mindfulness nurtures the wisdom of knowing things as they *truly are*, and keeps the knower from *being* carried away in the mechanics of activities, too far.

"Thereupon, when things are revealed and perceived as they really are: the right reception, ingestion, and reaction occurs without leaving behind impressions and scars.

"The flux of awareness is unbound and aligned with cosmic totality, and the one who surrenders to its stream swims deception-free.

"The secret of mindfulness is that the profit is cheaper than the loss; it's easier to keep the debris away than to practice mental floss."

Hearing this, a few moved closer to Shunyasati and said, "We are ready to make this mindful cup of tea. With determination in our hearts, could we be mindfulness devotees?"

Shunyasati smiled and spoke, "I can see the seed is sown with the right intention, and it is ready now to be watered with the right attention.

"First, unlearn the foolishness of the cities, and learn the wisdom of mountains, as they have the right attitude to make a river out of the pouring rains.

"Distrust the cities, who disrespect the rains, and let the water be flushed out recklessly in drains.

"They do not care for the rainfall, which gets lost in everything else and moves unnoticed and small.

"Street water in cities assumes the form of its function; with dirt, it is dirt, and with good, it becomes good, without any regulation.

"Whereas mountains shape up a sharp stream out of the rainfall, which flows downhill, humble, and wise and useful to all.

"Like the water, your awareness is mixed in all doing modes like knowing, thinking, feeling, or sensing in our living abode.

"Like the city, your forgetful *being* blends your awareness in its modifications carelessly. You become a consumer of experiences and reacts with witless sensations spontaneously.

"Whereas like a mountain, a mindful *being*, makes use of awareness as a sharp stream to reveal the nature of modalities, and still remembers it as distinct power from its functionalities.

"Mindfulness enables us to discriminate these modalities among themselves, and let the *being* witness these modes separate from the awareness of self.

"This discriminative realization dissolves the rigid image of ego by revealing the undercurrent of impermanence, that is always on the go.

"Therefore, O' Beloved, adopt the right attitude of the mountain's height and cultivate awareness to direct it on subjects as a steadfast stream of light.

"The stream flows down, but the mountains remain uninvolved; likewise, *equanimity* without manipulation is the protocol.

"With this right attitude, be the pure witness to the modifications, in the body and mind, and their patterns and configurations. And while witnessing, be conscious to remember yourself in the midst of all these acting members."

After this long commentary, Shunyasati looked at the devoted villagers and asked them to start making the tea.

He watched them with penetrating eyes and saw that they were sincere in learning the technique and eager to imbibe.

It was a new art of living that could not be understood merely by a thoughtful hack, but must be worked out earnestly, as a tactful knack.

So asked Shunyasati to the first villager, "What are you doing? Your hands are moving all random and reckless. That is not making the tea with mindfulness."

The first villager answered, "I am only mindful of my hand movements and their touch. Is this not enough for mindfulness, as such?"

Answered Shunyasati, "No, you are concentrating instead of witnessing the physicality of "knowing" that is only the 'what' aspect of the action. Add the mindfulness of thought by observing the 'how' aspect of the action.

"Inefficiency arises when 'what' and 'how' of an activity are not aligned, and mindfulness of these two makes us aware of our action's design.

"Beware—thoughts are powerful traps and steer you away from awareness of action and onto a journey of mindless lofty maps.

"Witnessing an action does not mean living-carefree or with reduction; it merely implies cooperation without *being* carried away in its addiction.

"So be mindful of 'what' and 'how' of its mechanics. Thus, be efficient at physical action by knowing its physics."

Then the tea maker turned to the second villager, who was working with precision as an expert, pouring the tea leaves and sugar grains and laboring as a robot with a straight and strained face.

"O dear, you looked stressed. Do you like this tea making?" asked Shunyasati.

Answered the second villager, "I have a clear awareness of my physical senses and the movement of thought but find no meaning in this barren act of filling the teapot. Does mindfulness watching mean, not enjoying the activity?"

The tea maker answered, "You are able to witness the 'what' and 'how' of the action, but without any feeling of 'why,' you lack any juice in your action.

"Purpose gets strength from meaning when it is felt in the heart, and without meaning, the activities pass by, as if you are a bionic cart.

"Thus, add the mindfulness of feelings in the actions, but be watchful, as they are very slippery and create reactions.

"Watch closely their patterns of appearance; and how they manipulate the mind to honor the sense of ego and self-importance.

"Also, they are the glue for the ingredients of delusion and suffering. As they hide in blind spots of your "self" as secret spies in the court of a king."

Shunyasati then moved to the third villager, who was working like an artist, full of purpose and motivation, but his face reflected worry, like the waves in a mist.

"You looked engaged but lost, fulfilled but consumed in a sort of a quiz. Are you trapped in your doer ship? Do you know who the tea maker is?" asked Shunyasati.

Spoke the third villager, "I am able to witness the physical sensations, thoughts, and feelings in my abode, but side by side, stress is spooling in me around these nodes. Why am I tense?"

Shunyasati answered, "Having understood the art of doing a mindful action, now is the time to shift awareness inward, toward the doer's function.

"This self-remembering is the subjective awareness of 'who,' without which you live with a false sense for what you do.

"Thus, a mindful action is mindfulness of doing and doer as one unit without fractions.

"Be aware that self-remembering is not an ego reminder. The former makes us unconditionally free, and the latter is a conditional binder.

"Self-remembering happens when the doer is filtered out of doing, whereas ego happens when the doer is born out of doing."

Thereupon Shunyasati moved towards the fourth villager, who was engaged and clearly at ease. A silent glow appeared on his face, and he mesmerized the villagers with his grace.

Shunyasati touched his feet, and with a humming heart and sparkling eyes, he moved around as if he had gotten his prize.

Said Shunyasati, "You have known the magic of mindfulness and emptied yourself of any "am-ness."

"With the "sati" of Shunya, you are now Shunyasati, and no longer will you need any teacher, toolkits, or this tea."

Hearing about his departure, the villagers froze, and with heavy hearts, they asked for his last sermon.

Shunyasati gazed gently around as if gliding in gratefulness and spoke,

"In the transactions of mind and matter; the *being* remains consumed and inevitably battered.

"To come out of this suffering, it blindly looks for solutions, and in doing so, it clings more to these transactions.

"You are pulled and pushed for something to which you don't truly belong, but you accept the worldly propaganda just because it looks so strong.

"But one day you will realize that your path is wrong, and you were singing loud only out of compulsion, for that which was never your heartfelt song.

"And on that day, when you feel your soul so strong, all compulsive noises will bow down before the sound of your inner gong.

"The mindfulness will amplify this dormant sound into words and words into actions, and this will make you aware of the chain of perceptions turning into mindful reactions.

"Thus, learn how to drive this mindfulness train; and free yourself from becoming victims of compulsive—pleasure or pain.

"In this train, your intention is the engine, and determination is the fire, with bogies of mind and matter tied together, through conscious wires.

"Thereupon, load or unload passengers—like perceptions, thinking, feelings, sensations, and impressions in it. But, first, make your awareness as the ticket checker to verify before letting them sit or exit.

"This awareness is neutral and does not make any ally or enemy, but focuses its light on revealing them to know their trip and identity.

"It maintains the *equipoise* and *equanimity* in the bogies, but itself remains relaxed, busy, and easy.

"Four are the key stations of this journey: first, learn the technique, second practice with mundane tasks, thirdly make it a lifestyle, and fourthly, uproot the miseries and their masks.

"Finally, be aware of that, any train is only a means to an end, and move beyond in existential oneness to blur and blend.

"May you all attain the 'sati' of Shunya and let the 'sati' merge in Shunya."

Thereupon, Shunyasati left the village with a glow and a smile.

Emptiness (Śūnyatā)

What is it:
Whose existence is its annihilation?
Whose knowing burns the knowledge?
Who cannot be held, though, is always in your hands?

Emptiness is its name.

Prelude

Emptiness is a great understanding and is most difficult as well. Its nature is non-dualistic and is fundamental for the duality to exist. It is not against any type of thing or thought but is a background beyond any "thingness." The potentiality of existence exists as *acausal* in it, makes it difficult to contemplate it—in terms of existence or nonexistence. But, it's OK not to contemplate, because emptiness is not a hypothetical theory to be studied, and be analyzed, to prove its nature. It is to be understood by seeing the nature of things in terms of their efficient cause, supporting causes, relative effect, and cessation, and looking behind the non-permanence of an involved phenomenon.

What is an efficient cause vs. a supporting cause? It is the primary cause of a phenomenon to occur. For example, for cooking—heat is the primary cause and utensils, stove, etc., are secondary causes. Since caveman to modern man, cooking needs heat, although supporting causes keep changing due to modernization to produce various relative effects. Caveman cooked on the wood fire and modern man prepares on gas appliances, but the heat as the efficient case remained the same. So, one needs to witness the background of efficient cause and effects by seeing their impermanence.

Emptiness is an active principle guiding meditators to go into the root of phenomenal *becoming* and uproot the efficient cause developing into a relative effect out of it. Because the cause is non-permanent, hence it is possible to eradicate it. For example, if a mindfulness meditator is working on a *painful feeling*, then he or she should keep going toward the efficient cause of that feeling, and eradicate the cause of that suffering in the body-mind framework.

Emptiness cannot be put in words or language, and, therefore, poses a great challenge to explain academically. The best way to describe it is with the negation principle, *what it is not*. Consequently, it can be said that it cannot be told but can be heard; it cannot be given but can be received. It seems illogical for an intellectual mind, but not for a mind who is able to see dualism in a phenomenon, and non-duality as its basis.

The primary reason for this difficulty is due to the limitation of our mental apparatus, which understands, remembers, and describes the experiences in terms of names and forms. And, generally, for any conversation to happen, we need a static reference point around which we build our understanding. Whereas, emptiness is a nameless experience, beyond forms, and basis for non-permanence.

Secondly, our learning is comparative, associative, and additive in nature. It is based on cause and effect relationships. Whereas, emptiness is neither the cause nor the effect in a phenomenon, and is beyond comparisons. Hence, the negation of any, thing or thought, is the best way to describe it.

Saying again, don't philosophize and over-analyze it, which may lead to wrong conclusions. Instead, dissolve into the phenomenon to the extent that the cause and effect chain is witnessed clearly, and free up awareness from both and their contents.

This short poem may sound illogical and against linear thinking because logic is base on inductive and deductive conclusions. It is only a pointer, but not a point itself, regarding emptiness. So, read it very slow to catch the meaning behind words.

Poem

Emptiness is not found in the gaps between things.
Emptiness is not created by removing things.
Emptiness is beyond the presence.
Emptiness is beyond the absence.
As absence is merely the sense of non-presence and exists against presence, and it is none.

Emptiness is not a quality of inertia in space.
Emptiness is not a quality of movement in space.
Emptiness is beyond the sense of space.
Emptiness is beyond the qualities of inertia and movement.
As inertia and movement are qualities to sustain a sense of space, and it is none.

Emptiness is not becoming new.
Emptiness is not remaining old.
Emptiness is beyond transitions.
Emptiness is beyond new and old.
As new is born out of old with its germs transformed, and it is none.

Emptiness is not a destination to pursue.
Emptiness is not holding upon some signs or clue.
Emptiness is beyond time and the path.
Emptiness is beyond calculations to do.
As a path, clues, and destinations are born out of time and its calculations, and it is none.

Emptiness is not a principle of Germination.

Emptiness is not a principle of Operation.

Emptiness is not a principle of Destruction.

Emptiness is beyond the principle of G.O.D.

As the G.O.D., the world has known merely is a personification of a principle, and it is none.

Emptiness is not to be worshiped.

Emptiness is not to be practiced.

Emptiness is beyond prayers.

Emptiness is beyond ritualistic gears.

As the worshiping is the chain of cause and effect and its linear bondage, and it is none.

Emptiness is not in knowing that I am part of a totality.

Emptiness is not in knowing that totality is an expansion of me.

Emptiness is not in knowing the border of self and non-self.

Emptiness is beyond the signs of a sense-sphere of a *being*.

Senses remember one and forget others, as one is against others, and it is none.

Emptiness does not flourish in the goodness of living.

Emptiness does not blemish with the pain of dying.

Emptiness is beyond living. Emptiness is beyond dying.

As dying and living evolve from each other, and it is none.

Emptiness does not arise by running away from things.

Emptiness does not vaporize by living lush like kings.

Emptiness is beyond fear.

Emptiness is beyond desire.

As fear is merely a sense of unfulfillment of desires, and it is none.

Emptiness is not a sweet saying, like "I love you."
Emptiness is not dead as well, without I and you.
Emptiness is beyond the crystals of I, Love, and You.
Emptiness is beyond the calculation of one plus one equals two.
As the meaning is hanging in words, and words are hanging in the gaps, and where is the gap hanging? And thus, it is none.

Emptiness is not a knowledge that can be transferred.
Emptiness is not a heritage that can be owned.
Emptiness is beyond the composition of one's effort.
Emptiness is beyond the imposition of a master to a follower.
As knowledge or heritage and to compose or impose are relative and directional, and it is none.

Emptiness is not a result of applied mental vectors.
Emptiness is beyond the application of feeling factors.
Emptiness is not a philosophy to comprehend.
Emptiness is beyond the doer ship of your hands.
As an *action,* this world has known born with "will" and its subjects, and it is none.

Emptiness can never be known by Your "self."
Emptiness can never be taught to Your "self."
Emptiness is beyond knowing.
Emptiness is beyond teaching.
Knowing and teaching is merely a library of Your "self's" consciousness, and it is none.

Emptiness is the essence of happening, empty of self.
Emptiness is the essence of knowing, empty of self.
Emptiness is the essence of meaning, empty of self.
Emptiness is the essence of quintessential, empty of self.
O' Beloved, May the *being* dissolve into emptiness and be empty of self.

Section 4

Four Step Meditation Technique

1. Knowing
2. Establishing
3. Mindful Living
4. Moving on and on

Prelude

In Buddha's tradition, there is a beautiful word called "Tathata," meaning—the way things really are. In its purest form, mindfulness is a practice of "Tathata"— to realize the way things are, as such. Some people translate "Tathata" as *suchness* in the English language.

Mindfulness enables a person to witness the *suchness* of objects (physical and mental), instead of getting occupied or carried away with them. It takes the direction from gross to subtle, forms to formless, names to nameless, and identity(s) to identity-less, awareness.

Let's elaborate on this understanding a little bit more.

At a gross level, one lives with a solid sense of "self" based on several identities created over time. These identities are composed of names and forms. These forms have qualitative and quantitative characteristics that give them meaning. And, this meaning is given a name. A human being, through perceiving, sensing, thinking, and feeling, is continuously engaged with names and forms to record experiences and also create new ones. In this way, we establish a linkage between self, identity, name-forms, and experiences.

In our daily practical life at a gross level, we perceive and memorize things, mostly with a fixed attitude of permanence. For example, we perceive that the nearest shopping mall is fixed, the home address is fixed, wall painting is fixed, and so on. Our belief in permanence becomes rock solid due to sameness in larger images of life. But look at things closely, the reality is very different. Now you enter the shopping mall for real, isn't it constantly changing with its content, pricing, people, noise level, lights, repair work, and so on. Whatever gives the meaning to a shopping mall is always in flux, and only its larger image is assumed to be static.

Similarly, when we observe ourselves at the gross level, we have a fixed idea of ourselves, but when we observe ourselves at a subtle level as such; we realize temporariness of experiences composed of names and forms. The identity related to them is also temporary, and the sense of self is also not solid. One realizes that *being* is a state and not a station in life. Also, when the *being* is mindful of "Tathata" or suchness of existential reality. The automatic flow of relaxation and wisdom occurs.

It is very promising, but how can we become mindful on it? Who holds the Intellectual Property of "Tathata" or mindfulness or anything like this? Where is the teacher from whom we can download this experience? Should we buy all the books and lectures on mindfulness?

Before we start running post to pillar, let's think upon these questions— Can an experience be taught? And, can the awareness of experience be thought? The answer is, 'No.' The experience, its awareness, and the sustaining of this quality is not an Intellectual Property. No one else has either ability to create your experience or right to own it.

One wonders then, why so many meditators speak and write about it? And, what is the use of tools, techniques, teachers, and teachings?

Let's look at the knowledge management aspects more minutely. There are three types of knowledge: tacit, explicit, and implicit.

- *Tacit knowledge* is personal wisdom coming out of experiential learning and internalization, which is difficult to codify, and share but is of greatest value in life.
- *Explicit knowledge* is an objectified skill, well structured, codified, and easy to share as a commodity.
- *Implicit knowledge* is somewhere hidden in translation between tacit to explicit.

Undoubtedly, mindfulness is *tacit* knowledge existing in the personal wisdom of a meditator's experience. The quality of awareness is only known to the meditator, which makes it subjective. At the same time, because we have a commonality in physical and mental structure to a certain degree. Few objective aspects can be explained using language indicators, which makes it *explicit* to a certain extent and few *implicit* points can be concluded as well. Therefore, it makes sense to learn it intellectually. Few tools and techniques can be codified, which can be a helpful aid to make progress. However, intellectual knowledge is useless until it is transformed into *being's* intelligence and personalized wisdom after practical application.

Additionally, mindfulness meditation is simple, universal, and result-oriented; therefore, it makes it a bit easier to write and speak about its methods.

For example, riding a bike is an experience one can only gain when he or she is actually riding it by continuously balancing and paddling to move on. Someone can write a book on *Riding a bike in 24 hrs.* In this book, one can explicitly elaborate on the precise algorithms, dos, and dont's required for riding. But, it cannot ensure that you can experience bike riding in 24hrs after reading it. What you need is a real bike, road, plus assessment of your situation. But the book can be helpful to give a checklist of things like helmet, brakes, seat adjustments and so on. In any case, before you start riding a bike you have to put down the book and go on your own. Because neither you can experience the ride while reading on your couch, nor you can read while riding the bike on the road. Secondly, you learn basic balancing and paddling on an isolated road rather than on a mountain terrain or a highway. But once you have discovered you can choose to go as advanced as you want. Learning mindfulness meditation technique is also similar to bike riding.

This chapter elaborates on a technique on how to cultivate mindfulness in four easy steps with a detailed map of each step. The reader should read it carefully step by step. If needed, re-read it but only for its practical significance instead of intellectual understanding. A learning map is also given in the beginning to provide a summarized version of the technique.

May we all live mindfully!

May we all experience "Tathata"!

Mindfulness Learning Map
—Step by Step

1. Foundational Discipline—Knowing
   - Basic self-inquiry and foundational learning
   - Equanimity and Equipoise
   - Models of mind and distraction management
   - Understand the role of concentration vs. mindfulness
   - Compose a mental torch—intention, attention, and awareness
   - Choose breath as an object of meditation
   - Cultivate discriminative awareness between objects and the field of awareness
   - Cultivate mindfulness of physical sensations, mental activity, and feelings
   - Realization of the ego as a non-entity and psychological complex

2. Develop Discipline into Deep Learning —Getting Established
   - Establish strong discipline and practice
   - Cultivate a discriminative awareness between forms and formlessness
   - Cultivate self-awareness by developing a sense of knowing oneself. It can also be called self-remembering
   - Cultivate clear comprehension of the unconditional nature of "self"
   - Learn to come out of deep mental states back to normal, during meditation

3. Transform Learning into a Lifestyle—Mindful Living
    - Cultivate mindfulness of dynamic activities, out of meditation room
    - Tailor social engagement philosophy/model for yourself while being mindful
    - Cultivate generosity, loving-kindness, and compassion qualities
    - Cultivate mindfulness quality as a lifestyle
4. Moving Beyond Mindfulness—Keep Moving On and On
    - Move beyond the milestones
    - Inner connectedness and surrender to existence
    - Living existentially as an experience instead of the experiencer

Four-Step Meditation Technique

Introduction

"Meditation" is a very widely used term nowadays. Its scope covers many scenarios: Concentration, Yoga, Mantra, Hypnosis, Chakra, Mudra, and other complicated occult techniques. This chapter neither approves nor criticize any form(s) of meditation. They may or may not be relevant in their respective use case scenarios.

The scope of this chapter is to precisely codify the steps required for mindfulness meditation in its simplest, practical, and result-oriented form. This technique is not rooted in any religion or ritual. Instead, it is a rational, mostly systematic, and activity-based technique. And, it is generically applicable to all. At the same time, it is not a motivational technique of *becoming* something, in terms of good or bad, winner or loser, strong or weak. Rather, it enables the meditator to realize the true nature of things in the body-mind framework and thus liberate the caught-up mind and enable it to live fresh and free.

The end goal is to cultivate clear comprehension, to free up the "awareness," which is caught up in subject (ego-self) and its object orientations, and purify the mind in a relaxed manner. The automatic outcome is a radical transformation of your *being*.

For the sake of simplicity, this technique is organized into four steps. And, each step is further organized into sub-steps—context, goals, supporting details (like posture, attitude, and so on), technique, procedure, and helpful progressive signs to move onto the next step.

The four steps are, as following:

- Learn the Foundational Technique and Discipline—Knowing
- Deep Learning and Develop Strong Practice—Getting Established
- Advance the Practice into a Lifestyle—Mindful Living

- Moving beyond Mindfulness—Keep Moving On and On

Keynotes on sub-steps:

- *Context* provides the background. Also, it helps in transitioning from one step to the next.
- *Goals* are guideposts only. The word "Goal" can be misleading, as someone can set unrealistic expectations, and continuously look for achievement certification during meditation. That will be counterproductive. Goals are required only to provide directional signs to the practice.
- *Supporting Details,* like postural guidelines, attitude, hints, tips, and other details, are specific to the step. These details help in preparing the right mindset, which in turn accelerates the practice. These can be shared between one or more steps. For example, the attitude described in Step#2 is also applicable to Step#1.
- *Technique* is the actual meditation activity to be performed, as stated in the given sequence. An important point to know is that during the meditation practice, the mind fluctuates into various mental states, which offers tempting reasons not to move on. This creates a deceptive understanding, which is counterproductive. In case of confusion, reread goals, and helpful signs.
- *Progressive signs* are symptoms aligned to goals. Their realization and acknowledgment indicate the meditator's mind to transition to the next step in a reasonable manner.

1. Learn the Foundational Technique and Discipline—Knowing

1.1 Context

A strong foundation is a prerequisite for meditation to flower. Doing meditation is a very well-thought-out application of effort and requires special attention. Therefore, it is necessary to understand the fundamentals of tools and techniques clearly.

The very first step is to know the common 7- Ws of mindfulness meditation and prepare accordingly. These 7-Ws are: Who, Why, What, Which, How (quantitative and qualitative measurements), Where, and When. It's a good idea to write it down formally in your diary with honest answers to all of these and keep revising it, as clearly as possible. These are explained in various parts of this book, and this chapter is also answering many of these 7-Ws. The most important thing i s the ability to tailor the knowledge as per your situation and bring efficiency in the effort to make it most effective for yourself. This personal learning is not an intellectual exercise but requires a real effort to create workable self-discipline. Therefore, be very reasonable based on your daily lifestyle and situation.

Secondly, this section will describe the basic techniques required for mindfulness of forms, both mental and physical. These forms include our thoughts, imaginations, feelings, sensations (pain, itching, hunger, body weight, and so on), vision, hearing, touching, tasting, and smelling. Spend a lot of time in gaining clarity on basics and building foundational discipline. The right discipline domesticates the mind's focus and energy for its appropriate usage.

1.2 Goals

1.2.1 Learn basic guidelines and tools

1.2.2 Build a foundational discipline

1.2.3 Establish discriminative awareness

1.3 Postural Guidelines

1.3.1 Choose a simple, stable, and comfortable posture. It should keep you alert and easy. You can sit on the ground, on a meditation pillow, or a chair. Use props as needed. It is better if you can sit with an upright spine. Keep checking your posture during the actual practice as well.

1.3.2 Before starting meditation, do a quick survey of your body from head to toes using your mind's eye. Make sure your head is stable on shoulders, eyes are soft—half or full closed, jaw muscles are loose, mouth is gently closed, neck muscles are soft, shoulders are loose, arms are near torso, hands are resting in the lap or on thighs, legs are relaxed, foot muscles are soft. Overall you should feel firm and relaxed.

1.3.3 Avoid changing postures frequently during meditation, but if needed, then adjust it slowly to ease pain or discomfort in any part of the body.

1.3.4 Do a few experiments to finalize your best posture. In the end, your posture should allow you to sit for approximately 60 minutes without agitating or tiring the body, and keep you alert, and non-drowsy.

1.4 Helpful Attitude, Alerts and Cues

1.4.1 Attitude

1.4.1.1 Cultivate the attitude of steady motivation (not impulsive passions), patience, and determination. Take it easy to consistently evolve in meditation—crawl, walk, and run.

1.4.1.2 Be curious and careful to explore the unknown territory. Remain engaged to experience, but do not expect any predefined result or imaginary goals.

1.4.1.3 Be sincere but not serious, jovial but not cheesy, watching but not judging, and be a carrier rather than a container of experience.

1.4.1.4 Cultivate simplicity and meaningfulness in day to day activities. How?

Simplicity occurs due to the alignment between mind, speech, and action. And, meaningfulness is ensured, when a sense of fulfillment is felt in the heart. On the contrary, engaging in prideful or meaningless gossips are not part of the meditator's daily activities.

1.4.1.5 In the beginning, every sitting could lead to a different result. It is not due to the wrong meditative effort, but mostly due to your sub- conscious or conscious mental states at that time. The most important thing to remember—not to alter, manipulate, create, or expect any other experience than what you are observing "now." Know that mindfulness meditation enables us to see the way things really are in the present moment, instead of what we wish them "to be."

1.4.1.6 Cultivate an attitude for direct and deep immersive experiences rather than calculated and superficial to suffice your intellectual understanding. In fact, before every session, it will be helpful to motivate yourself to immerse in meditation deeper than in the previous session.

1.4.2 Alerts

1.4.2.1 Be watchful of your consumption and associations in terms of both—physical and mental objects. Watch your food, thoughts, friends, and environment. Try to refrain from extremities of any kind. Avoid intake of anything which alters mental states.

1.4.2.2 Do not sustain a painful posture to prove physical success. Experiment with different postures to finalize your favorite posture for stable and comfortable sitting.

1.4.2.3 You should never feel a headache or light-headedness after mindfulness meditation.

1.4.2.4 These are clear signs that something is not going right. If this happens, stop, and re-align your efforts with the given procedures in this chapter.

1.4.2.5 After every meditation session, you should feel more composed, and clarified. If that is not the case, then re-examine your effort.

1.4.3 Cues

1.4.3.1 For motivation, it is good to find a company of other mindfulness meditators, but be watchful of not changing your own course, under any influence. The company should be constructive and gentle rather than disruptive for your effort. Do not engage in social dynamics and stay on course.

1.4.3.2 Pick up a competent and credible book on mindfulness and read a page or two before sleeping or in the morning. This will help in keeping your motivation up.

1.4.3.3 Check your moods and mental states a few times during the day. Realize how it changes over time as a result of meditative effort. Mental responses change tremendously, for good.

1.4.3.4 Keep a journal to record your meditation experience and read it occasionally to understand the graph of experiences.

1.5 Space and Schedule Management

1.5.1 In the beginning, it is essential to create an encouraging space for meditation to reduce distractions. The following instructions could be helpful:

1.5.1.1 Find an easily accessible, safe, clean, and quiet location.

1.5.1.2 Should be well aerated but avoid a windy place or use of strong fans.

1.5.1.3 An odor-free place is preferable. Refrain the use of perfumes, or incense, etc.

1.5.1.4 Light should be conducive to eyes. Do not use bright, colorful lights in the room.

1.5.1.5 Avoid "tick-tick" sound clocks Rather. Use a simple reminder bell, if needed.

1.5.2 A regular cadence and synchronized schedule is important in solidifying the discipline. The following instructions could be helpful:

1.5.2.1 Create a realistic and sustainable timetable. It should not become a burden or else it will fall below the priority line, among other daily activities.

1.5.2.2 Start with a short practice of 20 mins. Add 10 mins slowly and go up to 60 mins maximum. Remember, quality is more important than the quantity of effort.

1.5.2.3 Initially, a timer bell can help to track the period of effort.

1.5.2.4 Start with once a day and then switch to twice but avoid overdoing it.

1.5.2.5 Best time is morning, and evenings are equally good too but avoid late-night Meditations in the beginning. For some people, it can disturb sleep, which can be demotivating.

1.6 Equanimity and Equipoise

1.6.1 Our mind fluctuates all the time, and our default tendency is to be consumed and react immediately. However, in mindfulness meditation, from the get-go, we need to learn to witness and to regulate the reacting mind; by building the skill of equanimity.

1.6.2 It is required to cultivate a balancing force as a back-seat regulator of foreground fluctuations and not fall for them. Consider how a bird flies, it uses the two wings to fly and move up, but the third tail wing remains hidden, which provides the balance.

1.6.3 Equanimity is a necessary regulatory mental discipline to cultivate mindfulness. Without it, the meditator fills up a bottomless bucket. It doesn't matter how long someone is meditating for; the effort can become futile without equanimity.

1.6.4 Also, realize that equanimity is not a coercive way of regulation but a compassionate one. It is not required to pressurize yourself to be painful; instead, cultivate a deep understanding by witnessing fluctuations—arising, and vanishing; without an obsessed and compulsive reaction towards it.

1.6.5 Equanimity and the awareness torch (described later) create a special situation in the body-mind framework, which helps in nurturing the meditative effort to be distraction-free.

1.6.6 In general, equanimity is a great life skill. It saves us from many regretful acts which we might do out of rage, otherwise. It allows us the time necessary to think before we act.

1.7 Distraction Management of Thoughts, Feelings, and Sensations

1.7.1 Before exploring the strategies of distraction management, it is important to understand our mental states. We can have many mental states, but for easy understanding, let's use a simple model, as given in Raja Yoga by Sage Patanjali. He described five states, as following:

1.7.1.1 *Moordh Awastha*—Dull State. Characterized by low energy of intention, attention, and awareness. This results in mindlessness, low activity, and unclear perception.

1.7.1.2 *Kshipt Awastha*—Scattered state. The mental state is agitated and very chaotic, like a beehive of mental objects. Low intention and attention. Awareness is variably hyperactive but useless. This scattered state results in mindless drainage of energy. For example, in a stressful situation, the mind is haunted by many wild thoughts simultaneously and makes us tired, without purpose.

1.7.1.3 *Vikshipt Awastha*—Alternating mental state. Unintentionally, the mind travels between several thought-trains one after another, capturing your attention alternatively. The intensity of awareness remains variable, depending upon the associated mental objects of thought-trains. Over time, this becomes a strong habit, and its uncontrollable speed makes us slaves of our own mind. A negative thought-train can take us to a destination of depression very fast, or a self-appeasing thought-train takes us to a puffed-up destination.

Likewise, there are many destinations of this mental state with their respective pros and cons. In any case, we lose the mindfulness of the present moment. We invest ourselves in jobs, movies, sports, social media, and so on; to engage and enjoy alternate mental states without being mindful of them. Most of us live in this variability for our entire life. Interesting, isn't it?

1.7.1.4 *Aykagra Awastha*—Focused state. The mental state is steady due to the alignment between intention, attention energy, awareness, and object of meditation. Clarity of subject and object is gained.

1.7.1.5 *Nirudh Awastha*—State of Oneness. The mental state is unbound and free from discrimination of subject and objective consciousness.

The first three states—Dull, Scattered, and Alternating mental states— are more relevant to discuss distraction management. And, distractions are commonly caused by three mental constituents, namely: thoughts, feelings, and sensations. Let's talk on the power of these constituents and their distraction management strategies, one by one.

1.7.2 Distractions powered by thoughts, and their management:

Many meditators believe that one should strive to become thoughtless. The answer is, "No." Because meditative effort is not to suppress, exclude, and eliminate thoughts, but to be mindful of them.

Thoughts may be distracting but are very helpful links and pointers to our hidden closet of mind. Know that a thought can be the best interpreter of hidden and repressed behaviors in our known language. For example, if you are unfulfilled deeply inside, then your thinking, attitude, and reactions can provide the clue, and hook for it. Therefore, by examining the thoughts mindfully, you can reach to their origin. In this way, thoughts are helpful translators of the roots of your sufferings.

But the flip side is that the "thinking" becomes an addiction, making you an Obsessive-Compulsive Thinker, and distracts you in various degrees. And thoughts consume you, rather than you use them for any meaningful self- examination. Therefore, cultivating a gap between thoughts and observer is an investment which a meditator makes to use them for mindfulness. But a meditator should never force the mind to rejoice or reject any specific thought. This is achieved by remaining a passive observer instead of a driver of thoughts during meditation sessions.

Let's go a bit deeper. Our mind produces thoughts very fast, one after another like a nuclear reactor, and we keep chasing them mindlessly. Scattered thoughts arise and die like moving clouds, if you follow one cloud, winds can scatter it into thousands more, now which one to follow? Therefore, during meditation, a meditator should be aware of scattered and alternating mental states and should manage them as distractions, instead of following thoughts. How?

By non-cooperation and passive witnessing, these thoughts will be deprived of attention energy, and the mind will not react to reproduce many more thoughts. Don't alter or manipulate them by any force, they will drop by themselves. The mind will be decluttered like a blue sky.

Another situation is that sometimes self-talks may become strong mental traps, and can take us on the journey of self-pleasing, self-torturing, self-denying, or guilt trips. The mind keeps alternating from one trap to another. In these exceptional cases, "breath" is a good broom for thoughts. How?

When strong, superficial, and alternating thoughts make it impossible to come back to the object of meditation; then take a few deep, but conscious breaths, with retention—external and internal alternatively. And, do not cooperate with these thoughts or maybe open eyes halfway. Repeatedly remind yourself to come back to the breath, but do not change the locus of meditation. Remember to maintain passive equanimity.

Another situation is that when distracting thoughts are coming up from sub-conscious, either as continuous recordings from the past, such as songs or painful or pleasurable life episodes or uncoordinated thoughts in deep swings, such as images or memories. Let them arise and pass away, do not enjoy or exclude them in any way. Remember to maintain equanimity.

In summary, remember to befriend your mental states before regulating them. If disciplined correctly, our thoughts can become helpful messengers instead of distractions. The use of violent force to suppress them can be harmful, but the regulation of attention energy can help in understanding and breaking the habit patterns.

1.7.3 Distractions powered by feelings, and their management:

Like thoughts, our feelings are also very helpful messengers. Their messages provide insight into the roots of our reactions. Therefore, we do not want to paralyze our minds by suppressing them and become emotionless zombies. Rather, we need to work with them skillfully to sterilize them to help us in our meditative work, and not become distractions.

Feelings express themselves in a variety of weak or strong emotions. And, emotions mixed up with thoughts can become strong mental traps; strong enough to make us mindless. These traps can make us dull, miserable, hyperbolic, or over-excited. Also, sometimes feelings remain unexpressed or suppressed in the layers of mind, causing unknown anxiety and irritation. During meditation, both known and unknown feelings can cause distractions and need to be managed. How?

When a feeling arises, put the torch of awareness (described later) on it, and stay tuned to directly perceive it by filtering out thoughts from it. Examine its degree of strength, for example, if strong jealousy is arising, clearly observe it, and honestly remind yourself, "I am modified into strong jealousy now," and witness it's going away. Remind yourself that jealousy is dying now.

For superficial feelings, continuous reminders to return on the object of meditation is enough.

But sometimes feelings are like floodwater and require a dam to be built to hold them. How?

For strongly negative feelings, use the association of positive feelings as an antidote to weaken them. Once they've been countered, then drop the positive feelings as well. For example, when anger arises, associate it with affection to curtail it, and then drop affection as well. It is also known as "Pratipaksha Bhavana" in yogic traditions. It is said that "when disturbed by negative thoughts, the opposite should be cultivated." Likewise, for strong pleasurable feelings self-regulation and restrictive feelings act as an antidote.

Also, sometimes negative feelings can be subtle, internally driven, and not tied to any clear thoughts. They create unreasonable crankiness and frustrations in us. This can be due to our repressed and residual painful experiences, grounded in the sub-conscious mind. These unexpressed feelings are psychological landmines, waiting for someone to step on and make us explode. In this case, the mind tries to find external excuses to create justified labels of thoughts for our hidden negative feelings, which could be irrational. For example, the mind works to blame someone for its anger and guilt; to look reasonable for its inner irritation. In this scenario, initially, equanimity is helpful, but later, meditation of loving and kindness is the real remedy.

Mindfulness meditation is the antidote for a dramatic mind; therefore, a little progress should weaken the strength of negative feelings and help you to move on. In short, a few sessions of sincere meditation will automatically minimize the irrational modifications of the mind.

1.7.4 Distractions powered by sensations, and their management:

Sensations supply the building materials to our experiences and trigger our reactions.

They arise with other associated aspects. It could be either physical like hunger, heat, cold, pain, tingling, itching, and so on or mental like anger, pride, jealousy, passions, and so on. But in all cases, their currency is in three denominations—either pleasurable, un-pleasurable, or neutral sensations.

They play a significant role in our choice-making because we desire for pleasurable sensations and avoid un-pleasurable ones. In this way, our preferences, attachments, and aversions about things and situations are pivoted around sensations.

During mindfulness meditation, one finds that sensations play a lot of games. Suddenly somewhere, it starts itching, or you feel hungry, or restlessness or other mental sensations may arise.

This may distract and drive you crazy, making it hard to meditate. You may not find this difficulty at all while watching a two-hour movie, sitting on the sofa. Why does this happen? Remember, movie watching or other entertainments are passionate engagements, whereas mindfulness is unconditional witnessing inside you. This is a new mode, your body- mind is learning, and old habit patterns tend to react and oppose due to previous attachments and aversions. In mindfulness, you do not attach or avoid, but witness what is happening. So, how to deal with the distracting sensations?

Equanimity is the regulator of distractions due to sensations. Watch the arising sensation, maintain the equanimity, and watch it dying without reacting. This is the practice to weaken the power of sensations. Within a few *sittings,* you will realize these distracting sensations are no more influencing your effort, and you are progressing. If a sensation is excruciating, gently act upon it to remediate it, in addition to equanimity; and return to your meditation.

1.8 Concentration and Mindfulness, side by side

Both concentration and mindfulness are important meditation skills, lead us to different qualities in mind. Although concentration skill is not the prime objective of this chapter, it feels necessary to talk a bit about its meaning, role, and position in comparison to mindfulness.

1.8.1 Definitions

Concentration (*Aykagra Awastha*), is a singular and focused mental state as explained in (1.7.1.4.) This mental state is attained by zooming into the object of meditation by progressively excluding or suppressing any other fluctuation in mind. It is dependent on will, circumstances, and the object of meditation. Accordingly, it has advantages and disadvantages.

Suppose a kid desires to play her favorite video game. She goes to her room, closes the door, puts on the headphones, switches on the TV, and starts playing. Thereupon, her mind, physical senses, and reactions are tuned with the game, in a way that she and the game have become one system.

She has attained a concentrated mental state, conditioned with the game. Now she does not care for her food, homework, or anything that happens in the world. As a result, she has gained some mind skills and lost relaxation by negatively hurting her eyes. And, if you ask her to stop the game, she may have withdrawal symptoms like anger or frustration.

It is a story of mindless concentration that commonly exists in the human world in all ages, in various degrees.

Mindfulness meditation also requires some degree of concentration, but it is not of the type as described above in kid's video game example. Meditators are neither careless of the world nor of themselves. In a real sense, mindfulness is pure attention energy, inclusive of anything coming in its radar. For example, if a negative thought arises, one will witness negativity and be equanimous, and if a positive thought arises, one will witness positivity and be equanimous. There is no welcoming or withdrawal attitude created for specific experiences.

Let's explore dissimilarities, similarities, and role of concentration in mindfulness meditation.

1.8.2 Dissimilarities between concentration and mindfulness are, as following:

1.8.2.1 Concentration is best achieved when mental state is attached with the object of meditation, whereas mindfulness is best achieved when mental state is free from the object of meditation. Although it observes the object of meditation as a life cycle. There is a gap perceived, between subject and object, due to witnessing.

1.8.2.2 Concentration can result in withdrawal symptoms, whereas mindfulness is never attached to begin with. Many yogis become angry if someone disturbs their meditation because they desire concentration but feel withdrawn by disturbance. Therefore, they get easily annoyed and frustrated by withdrawal. It is not the case with a mindfulness meditator.

1.8.2.3 In concentration you reach out to the object, superimpose, and narrow down your focus on it, whereas in mindfulness, you are receptive of the object and let it reveal to you, fully.

1.8.2.4 Concentration is powered by will and active engagement, whereas mindfulness is ability to attend and witness with passive engagement with the object of meditation.

1.8.2.5 Concentration exists by conditions, whereas mindfulness can be unconditional. Former is always object-oriented, but the latter could be objectless.

1.8.3 Similarities between concentration and mindfulness are, as following:

1.8.3.1 Both are mental states and require a diligent practice to achieve successful results. These both are important for discriminative awareness (explained later).

1.8.3.2 Concentration provides the reference point upon which the attention is fixed, and mindfulness offers insight into the nature of things. Both provide knowledge of things, though in different ways.

1.8.3.3 Both concentration and mindfulness can bring tranquility. However, the qualities could be different. The former is unstable, and the latter is stable. How? Tranquility due to concentration is like a ball balanced on an inverted bowl, a slight movement can throw it off, and needs will power to put it back, whereas tranquility due to mindfulness is like a ball sitting inside the bowl, even after getting shaken; it will settle down again into its position as a natural course.

1.8.4 Role of concentration in mindfulness meditation

1.8.4.1 A reasonable degree of concentration is helpful in supporting and establishing mindfulness. It aids in sustaining the focus during meditation.

1.8.4.2 Concentration helps pass through the three mental states as described earlier: dull, scattered, and alternating. The basic arrangements described earlier, like finding a silent room, bell timer, early morning session, and so on, are attempts to create the right circumstances for a focused mental state.

1.8.4.3 Mind needs a certain reference point to understand that it is distracted and what is the degree of distraction. Concentration can be a measurement and alignment tool.

1.8.4.4 A concentrated mind with positive mental factors allows for pleasant and calm mental states. It indicates that meditation is working in the right direction. Therefore, concentration skills are helpful if applied in the right manner and attitude. One needs to understand its nature and usage clearly.

1.9 Cultivate Discriminative Awareness between Object and the Field of Awareness

To make mindfulness skills sharper, the first and foremost step is to perceive distinctly between the object(s) of experience and the field of awareness. And, to achieve it, we need to cultivate a mental quality of intention, attention, and awareness. Let's call this quality as "mental torch." To make this torch effective and efficient, one needs to practice it with a suitable object of meditation, like "Breath." The following sections will describe the technique to attain discriminative awareness in detail.

1.9.1 Composition of a mental torch—Intention, Attention, and Awareness of Object of meditation

These three qualities are used to compose a mental torch to be used upon an object of meditation. These qualities act as lenses of a camera and get adjusted in various stages to align meditative efforts. Let's discuss one by one.

1.9.1.1 Intention—Our normal consciousness modifies itself into various forms of experiences. For example, perception, thought, memory, image, or feeling. Intention localizes our consciousness and acts as the director of its modification.

1.9.1.2 Sustained attention—This is applied energy to keep oneself moving in an acquired or intended direction. Its strength determines the ability to flush out distractions.

1.9.1.3 Awareness—Awareness provides the field in which experiences occur. It can be compared to light in a room that allows objects to be seen. We use our awareness to experience various objects of meditation. It will be much clearer as we go forward.

1.9.2 Choose an object of meditation—Breath

For many obvious benefits, the breath is a good meditation object, initially. A detailed understanding of breath is provided in the chapter "Breathe to know." Few are given below as well:

1.9.2.1 Breath is easily accessible in all circumstances and times.

1.9.2.2 Breath can be volunteer and non-volunteer.

1.9.2.3 Breathing influences physical and mental body, and vice-versa. It's a natural and non-competitive process. It does not form a psychological ego—superiority or inferiority complex.

1.9.2.4 Breath can lead us into very deep states of meditation and can help in coming back to a natural state. The process of exiting out of deep meditative states using breath is described later (**#2.5.11**).

1.9.3 Cultivate a mental tool of discriminative awareness

After learning about mental torch, and choosing an object of meditation in previous sections, let's begin the meditation work using a simple procedure.

1.9.3.1 Be ready to sit for about forty-five minutes in a carefully chosen location, as described earlier (#**1.3**).

1.9.3.2 Sit in a firm posture with closed or half-closed eyes and do not focus on any specific thing. Keep your eye's muscles soft and relaxed.

1.9.3.3 Do a quick mental survey of your physical body to ensure there is no tightness due to posture, starting from the top of the head, forehead, face muscles, jaw muscles, ears, neck, trunk, hands, fingers, legs, feet, and toes. If there is any tightness, relax it.

1.9.3.4 Resolve in your mind to retain body/mind posture. In case it becomes difficult to maintain, change it with slow movement to attain easy posture.

1.9.3.5 Remind yourself to be alert, relaxed, and committed to this effort.

1.9.3.6 With closed eyes survey the surrounding space. Notice: sounds from far to near, smells, temperature, your body weight, and touchpoints with the ground.

1.9.3.7 Slowly bring the mental torch around the nostril's area and then on respiration. In the initial stages, it may be helpful to start by taking a few voluntary deep breath movements. Watch the movement, and then slowly change the breath; to be simple, soundless, and automatic.

1.9.3.8 Gently tune into the automatic breathing and try not to drive it. Keep tuning in until the awareness is reasonably merged with respiration.

1.9.3.9 Thereupon, start feeling the respiratory sensations in the nostrils. Keep the mental torch in this area, and feel the flow, temperature (cold-in & warm-out), moistness, and a touch of the air.

1.9.3.10 Slowly sharpen the ray of awareness by narrowing it on the area where the sensation is felt the most and sustain it for some time to experience the finer sensations.

1.9.3.11 The visualization of the location of sensation in the nostrils can be helpful. If there is any residual respiratory sound occurring, then tune in to it to be fully engaged.

1.9.3.12 Keep it a soft, passive, and sustained observation to become aware of real feelings and sensations of the touch. Do not conceptualize, imagine, or think about it.

1.9.3.13 Synchronize the mental torch and breath sensations going in and flowing out. Your mind may try to modify awareness into many other things and defocus, but gently come back to this synchronization. (Read section# **1.7** on distraction management).

1.9.3.14 Use this synchronization to know the key nodes: beginning, sustaining, and ending of sensation and gaps in between sensations.

1.9.3.15 Make a cadence to do this exercise regularly and create a synchronized mental-tool of intention, attention, and awareness to be applied on chosen sensation, in the nostril area.

1.9.3.16 Do this repeatedly, enough to become comfortable in using this mental torch to immerse in different respiratory sensations. Remember not to expect, alter, imagine, or create any experience.

1.9.3.17 This meditation will cultivate a perception of discriminative awareness between the object of meditation and field of awareness.

1.10 Establish Discriminative Awareness

The perception of discriminative awareness, between breath sensation and the field of awareness, is a key sign of readiness to move on to the next level of establishing it with other objects of meditation, like physical sensations, thinking, and feelings.

In day to day life, our body-mind framework does physical, mental, and their interrelated psychosomatic activities. Consequently, we experience them associated with sensations. These activities happen at conscious levels and sub-conscious levels. Let us begin by exploring them at a conscious level with different objects of meditation.

The basic meditation process remains the same, in the sense that it enables us to discriminate the awareness from objects of meditation—Physical or Mental. This mental state is no longer caught up in objects, and the meditator is no longer moving along with the objects. Secondly, it affirms that the mind has gained a certain degree of both skills—concentration and mindfulness.

In this way, the mental state of "Discriminative Awareness" is called as the real beginning of meditative states.

The following three sections are dedicated to cultivating discriminative awareness using sensations, thinking, and feelings; as various objects of meditation.

1.10.1 Meditation on Physical Sensations

1.10.1.1 What is a physical sensation? It can be anything felt on the body like—itching, pain, twitching, tingling, heaviness, heat, cold, dry, moist, movement, sweatiness, pain, hunger, and so on. These can be felt superficially on the skin or internally in the body, but we always experience sensations in our physical framework. Each form of sensation is experienced in the present moment, has a beginning, and an end. This momentary experience can be pleasurable, painful or neutral. And, we react to these sensations according to our likes and dislikes. Thereby, we form a peculiar and solid attitude of attachments and aversions towards sensations; in our self-hood.

1.10.1.2 After knowing about sensations, let's begin the meditation exercise. Do several dedicated meditation sessions on physical sensations, to gain their clear perception.

1.10.1.3 Read basic guidelines from previous sections (#**1.3-1.7**) if needed.

1.10.1.4 Begin with examining the body as one large unit of mass and cultivate awareness of how it feels right now as a whole body and about yourself.

1.10.1.5 If you should give a name about the sensation of your entire body-feeling, what will you say? Right now, I am feeling, either pleasurable or non-pleasurable or indifferent.

1.10.1.6 Sustain this awareness of generic sensation felt in the body as a whole for some time.

1.10.1.7 Thereupon, start examining the body parts in a sequence. To do it, create your personal sequence. The sequence and direction can be top to bottom or vice-versa and peripheral skin to internal organs.

1.10.1.8 Common sequential circuits are head to toe or vice-versa; right hand to left side covering the front body or vice-versa. Choose any one but survey the body in its entirety.

1.10.1.9 Common direction is out to in, during the scanning of the body parts. Start with sensations appearing or disappearing on the skin and then move inside to catch sensations in the internal body parts.

1.10.1.10 Let's begin by surveying the larger body parts—head, face, neck, shoulders, arms, hands, fingers, trunk, back, pelvic area, legs, foot, and toes—in a sequence, and with each part, be aware of sensations. Notice any prominent sensation. Realize the experience: pleasurable, non-pleasurable, or neutral.

1.10.1.11 Sustain the mental torch (intention, attention, and awareness) for just enough time to know the sensation, but not for a longer time to get caught into its experience. Then, move on to the next part quickly. The most important point is to witness the bare sensations without getting engaged in their pleasurable or un- pleasurable factor. In short watch sensations—part by part, one at a time, and remain equanimous in attitude.

1.10.1.12 Do it for few cycles and complete the circuit several times in one *sitting*. In the beginning, one can dedicate the entire mediation session, just up to this point for a few days.

1.10.1.13 Once you get the hang of it then in the same sequence, zoom into the body parts and narrow down the scope of examination to smaller areas. For example, while examining the face, explore forehead, right cheek, left cheek, nose, skin between the nose and upper lip, upper lip, lower lip, chin area, and so on. Again, notice the sensation just enough to know its nature and move on. Do not engage in it.

1.10.1.14 Do it for a few sessions until you are able to watch sensations in a narrow zone and clearly be aware of arising and dying of sensations on the body.

1.10.1.15 Now, in the same sequence, examine the physical body but move internally this time. Watch the joints, muscles, and internal organs. For example, start head to toe again—inside the skull, behind the eyes, inner ear canals, jaws, teeth, tongue, neck, shoulders, heart, liver, and so on.

Examine the skeletal system of your body, including the spine and its vertebrae, and a sense of the weight hanging around the spine. Be aware of sensations appearing and disappearing.

1.10.1.16 Do this for several sessions.

1.10.1.17 Once you've thoroughly examined the entire physical framework and sensations in sequence, leave the sequence, and do it in symmetrically opposite directions. For example, examine right- hand fingers, then examine left hand fingers, then examine hands, arms, and so on in opposite and symmetrical pairs. Remember your inner torch; keep moving it left to right and front to back.

1.10.1.18 Also, by this time mind would have gained skill of equanimity, therefore increase the time to watch bare sensations. And, know the root and boundary of sensation, with clarity as it is arising and dying away. For example, if your chest feels heavy, try to deepen the awareness where it reaches maximum heaviness, and widen the awareness where its lightness spread; to know where its root and boundary are. Also, observe its life cycle if it is arising, sustaining, or dying away.

1.10.1.19 Perform it for several sessions.

1.10.1.20 In the end, the meditator should be aware and able to watch the physical body as a body of sensations and not through a calculative sequence.

1.10.1.21 As a result, an insightful discriminative awareness is cultivated, that physical sensations are occurring in the field of awareness.

1.10.2 Meditation on Thinking and Thoughts

1.10.2.1 What is thinking? And, what is a thought? Thinking is a time-sensitive process based on memory, images, associations, logic, conclusions, and so on. This occurs in short sprints or long marathons. And, thoughts are outcomes or events of the thinking process. Our brain is continuously cooking thoughts in the form of ideas, opinions, judgments, concepts, and so on.

Although thinking is an activity happening in the present moment, it is dependent mainly on past or future thoughts, and on underlying conditioning of the mind. While doing meditation, a common but immediate observation will be that "thinking" and "witnessing" are inversely proportional to each other because both processes are occurring in the "present" moment, and the mind will supply attention energy to one at a time. Consequently, if "witnessing" is strong, "thinking" will become weak and vice-versa. This makes it challenging to do mindfulness meditation on the thinking process. It needs patience, so never try to curtail or control thoughts, by force.

1.10.2.2 After knowing about "thinking" and "thoughts," let's begin the meditation. Do several dedicated full sessions on thinking and thoughts to gain clear perception.

1.10.2.3 Read basic guidelines from previous sections#**1.3-1.7** if needed.

1.10.2.4 Begin with the examination of mental activities using the mental torch.

1.10.2.5 Let's begin by examining the thoughts—beginning, ending, and continuity. The continuous stream of thoughts with the cooperation of feelings maintains the velocity of thinking. If the meditator doesn't cooperate with thoughts and remains equanimous towards the feelings, the stream will dry out and will slow down "thinking." It will start inducing gaps between the thoughts.

1.10.2.6 Keep examining the patterns, associations, repetitions, strength, and flow of thoughts. Also, keep your focus on gaps between the thoughts.

1.10.2.7 If you are doing it correctly, the gaps between your thoughts will increase automatically. And, you will notice further slowing down of thinking.

1.10.2.8 Shift the mental torch on the feelings, underlying the thoughts and remain equanimous towards them, and move again to related thoughts.

1.10.2.9 This meditation will allow you to gain insight into your thoughts, which are building blocks of conditioning, and in turn, your attitude. After doing this meditation for several days, one can know that myriad thoughts sketch the self-concept. The "self" is a thought complex.

1.10.2.10 Perform it for several sessions.

1.10.2.11 At the end meditator should be aware and able to watch thoughts, their boundary, and gaps in between.

1.10.2.12 An insightful discriminative awareness is cultivated that thoughts are occurring in the field of awareness, and their continuity is thinking.

1.10.2.13 Note: If at any time it becomes impossible to watch your thoughts which can be due to the intensity of thinking, move back to breath awareness before returning to the thoughts as the the object of meditation.

1.10.3 Meditation on Feelings

1.10.3.1 What is a feeling? It is a mental sensation in terms of the "feel" factor of mental activity.

For example, emotions like anger, jealousy, joy, guilt, and so on; can have their distinct "feel" factors in the body. Like a physical activity leads to physical sensations or feeling, a mental activity triggers mental sensation or feeling. Also, the physical and mental body are inter-related. For example, intense anger as a feeling can even trigger the body to tremble, or mental stress can create tightness in the shoulders.

1.10.3.2 After knowing about feelings, let's begin the meditation. Do several dedicated full sessions on mental feelings to gain clear perception.

1.10.3.3 Read basic guidelines from previous sections (#**1.3-1.7.**) If needed.

1.10.3.4 Let us begin by examining the experience of mental sensations or feelings associated with thoughts. Adjust your mental torch to zoom into the feelings, to a level where you can observe the feelings separate from thoughts. Notice that feelings exist with thoughts, but can exist without thoughts, as well; for example, one can be sad without active thinking of the experience. In this case, this feeling will trigger sad thoughts. The mental activities can be circular in the sense that thoughts can trigger feelings, and vice-versa. Remember that feelings provide the gluing force for thoughts to associate with other thoughts and images. You can be feeling angry and look for thoughts to justify it, or on the contrary, some passionate thoughts can trigger angry feelings in your mind.

1.10.3.5 Examine the center and periphery of these feelings, including their strength, their arising, and dying out. Use discriminative awareness to watch feelings separate from underlying thoughts.

1.10.3.6 Examine the mental feeling triggering a physical sensation. For example, on a bad day, sad feelings may make your entire body heavy, and you may want just to lie down. But as a meditator, you do not simply react to this feeling by lying down. Instead, sit erect, watch, and be aware of its root, periphery, and movement. Also, examine the physical sensation, and try to find its cause in a mental feeling. This can happen due to stress. For example, you may have a tight and painful shoulder blade and neck due to a stressful issue in life.

1.10.3.7 Examine mental feelings for a considerable time in various meditation sittings.

1.10.3.8 This should further establish discriminative awareness and provide an experience that awareness is distinct but is also integrated with other faculties.

1.11 Helpful Progressive Signs

1.11.1 Discriminative awareness of body-mind faculties is experienced, and established in terms of physical sensations, mental activities, feelings, and their interrelationships.

1.11.2 *Being* is not clutched in compulsive tendencies of mental factors, and thus natural serenity and calmness are experienced in day to day life. Relief from anxiety and stress is realized.

1.11.3 Ability in regulating the mental torch upon the body-mind framework is attained.

1.11.4 Ability to remain equanimous/equipoise upon reactions, is attained.

1.11.5 Rigidity of the ego gets loosened. This results from realizing that the ego is a non-entity and a psychological complex. This realization is supremely important at this stage.

1.11.6 By now, you should be able to realize that thoughts, feelings, and sensations make up our experiences and consequently create impressions. As impressions become deep, they become solid patterns. The realization of these impressions and patterns results in deep learning.

1.11.7 Until now, the meditator has learned the building blocks of experiences. The next step is to learn from the experiences deeply and develop a strong practice. Let this learning become a portal to go much deeper into oneself.

2. Deep Learning and Develop a Strong Practice—Getting Established

2.1 Context

Our awareness flows naturally outward towards the worldly objects, through the doors of senses. In the previous section, the effort was in alignment with this natural flow because you cultivated object-oriented mindfulness, though at a superficial level. Again, these objects were: breath, sensations, thoughts, and feelings.

In this section, we will learn to develop a strong practice by building upon previous efforts and gain insight into the nature of objects of meditation by moving towards their roots.

Secondly, we will learn to turn objective awareness into subjective awareness, which can be called self-remembering. In this way, one can cultivate the mindfulness of awareness itself. This will bring deep learning and insight into the nature of the unconditional self.

2.2 Goals

2.2.1 Establish a strong discipline.

2.2.2 Cultivate a deep awareness of gaps between physical and mental objects.

2.2.3 Cultivate self-remembering by turning awareness towards the sense of knowing "oneself."

2.2.4 Cultivate clear comprehension of the unconditional nature of the self.

2.3 Postural Guidelines

2.3.1 Same as given in section#**1.3**.

2.4 Helpful Attitude, Alerts and Cues

2.4.1 Attitude

2.4.1.1 Read attitude section# **1.4**, and adopt as necessary, in addition to given below.

2.4.1.2 A strong practice is developed by remaining engaged, motivated, and connected to meditation's values and goals. It is important to understand and articulate your life values—both core and peripheral, and align them with practicing from the get-go. Secondly, the goals should not be bookish and massively arduous but should be simple, practical, and clear. Focus on incremental values instead of making far- reaching goals, aligned to your approach. Think i ncrementally, h ow mindfulness meditation will transform your daily life, instead of big goals like after-life or enlightenment or psychic powers type.

2.4.1.3 Sincerely prioritize meditation over other daily activities. This is another reason to do it first thing in the morning and then start your workday.

2.4.1.4 Remember the results seen in daily practice and contemplate on them. This motivates you to increase the intensity and keep you focused. Writing a journal can be a good thing, as well.

2.4.1.5 Be ready to move more deeply into subjective awareness and also of objective awareness via senses.

2.4.1.6 Keep an open and flexible mind to be able to switch the objects of meditation.

And in general, do not hang up too much with anything in life. Take it easy—let things come and go, in and out of life.

2.4.1.7 No habit is a good habit to cultivate. However, in case, some solid bad habits hinder the practice, then counter them with good habits, and later leave the good habits as well. As said by wise people, if a thorn is pinched in the foot, use another one to pull it out, but after that, both are useless.

2.4.1.8 Self-care and Self-management are extremely important skills to develop a strong and disciplined practice.

2.4.2 Cues

2.4.2.1 Mindfulness meditation realigns the three modes of consciousness—waking, dreaming, and sleep. With a regulated discipline of these modes, we can deepen the practice. The excess of anything is bad. For example, sleep is equally essential as wakefulness.

2.4.2.2 During wakefulness, maintain a self-caring, healthy, and happy discipline. Be mindful and restrictive of sharp emotions, feelings, and indulgences of food or physical sensual activities.

2.4.2.3 During sleep, maintain the right quota of sleep to create a refreshing and restful state. It is good to develop relaxing circumstances by making evenings lighter and peaceful.

2.4.2.4 In case nightmares come, say a compassionate prayer before sleeping, and you will see great results. Nightmares are uncommon for disciplined meditators, though.

2.4.2.5 Be mindful that your practice allows you to witness physical sensations, feelings, and thoughts distinctly, and distractions are reduced increasingly. If not, then keep working on distraction management from the previous section.

2.5 Procedure

2.5.1 Begin with witnessing the life cycle of physical sensations—origin, sustenance, end, gap, and re-occurrence. Now, focus the mental torch on gaps instead of sensation out of this life cycle.

2.5.2 In another session, witness thoughts and witness the widening of the gaps. By this time, thoughts should be subsidized. Focus the mental torch on silent gaps instead of thoughts.

2.5.3 In another session, witness feelings associated with or without thoughts. Focus the mental torch on gaps instead of feelings.

2.5.4 In short, develop the witnessing of widening gaps in terms of silence and emptiness. It is an important realization and very different from the previous step. In the previous step, the mental torch was on objects, and now it is focused on gaps in between the objects.

2.5.5 With this awareness of silence, use your mental torch to realize the complete cycle of experience by watching in the following manner:

2.5.5.1 Arising of experience (center) and fading away from experience (periphery).

2.5.5.2 Turning points of appearing and disappearing experience.

2.5.5.3 Gaps between the two: sensations, thoughts, or feelings of experiences.

2.5.5.4 Remaining equanimous about the urge to react out of an experience.

2.5.6 Take one objective experience at a time and complete the cycle. The gaps between objects will widen up, and objects will look like moving icebergs in a river.

2.5.7 Clearly comprehend discriminative awareness between forms and formlessness or gaps.

2.5.8 Establish deeply into this insight. It is a fundamental realization. Prepare to turn the mental torch towards the source of awareness in "you" instead of objects. Consequently, it becomes clear that awareness is the distinct but associative faculty for the experience to occur. And, a natural insight about the body and mind, cultivates in this self-awareness. Establish this practice very deeply.

2.5.9 This can also be called as discriminative awareness between objective and subjective consciousness. It can be developed further by doing the following:

2.5.9.1 Withdraw your torch away from any objects of meditation into the meta-sense of "knowing" instead of knowledge of objects and turn it inward. In other words, realizing the sense of pure knowing agnostic of objectified knowledge. (Difficult to write, tell or understand conceptually but easier to do once one has come to this stage of discrimination).

2.5.9.2 Let the purity of awareness stand by itself without any object. If any mental object comes up, then notice it and let it pass, but sustain the subjective awareness instead of getting involved in the phenomenon. This is unconditional awareness. Even though mental objects are appearing, awareness is no longer interested in participation with them.

2.5.9.3 Work on this practice until it becomes natural, and you get the hang of this turning point.

2.5.9.4 This unconditional awareness could become the center of observation, and you can witness objects around you, and it can be named as self-remembering or self-awareness.

2.5.10 In self-remembering, the attention is stronger on the subject than on any object. In this stage of meditation, the attitude toward sensations is, as follows:

2.5.10.1 Be deeply aware of bare sensations in the field of self-awareness without the need to know its cause, type, form, or location in the body. And, be aware of it's happening and disappearing in the field of awareness. Like a bubble appearing and disappearing in the ocean, when it happens, awareness of it arises; and when it does not occur, there is no awareness of bubble, although it is part of the ocean always.

2.5.10.2 A clear comprehension shows that awareness and objects together form experiences of the mind-body framework; thereupon, being aware of awareness without any object, sustain this pure awareness.

2.5.10.3 With this awareness, the discrimination of experience and experiencer is attained. Establish this practice of knowing the objects and subject; and be easy in turning gears, as you grow deep into it. It is crucial to be well-acquainted with this unconditionality and subjective awareness.

2.5.10.4 Note: Self-remembering is a deep state meditation where the mind is attuned in awareness, firmly. It is essential to understand entering and exiting out of it. Avoid any experimentation to jump out, accidentally out of deep meditations.

2.5.11 A valid and most important question arises, how would one come out of deep meditative states that are pure awareness or objectless or of intense concentration types or nature? Following are the cues:

2.5.11.1 If the meditator's mind is using a formal object of meditation and is mindful of it, then this section is not much relevant, as mind is bound to a form and is on the periphery. The momentum of the object is dynamic and will pull the meditator out with the easy and slow application of intention and waiting for some time.

2.5.11.2 If the mental state has moved into pure awareness or is in a deeply concentrated state and very few objects of fluctuation are arising, then read it carefully, as a sudden jerk could be harmful to your mind and its culture developed thus far.

2.5.11.3 If your mind has moved into deep meditation, then begin with mindfulness of your vital vibrations (a.k.a pranas in Sanskrit) to prepare for exiting out of meditation. For example, abdominal pulse. Sustain awareness for some time.

2.5.11.4 Thereupon, slowly tune mindfulness to the vibration of breath associated with pulse vibrations. The breath should be very slow and rhythmic in this state.

2.5.11.5 Sustain awareness on this slow-moving breath, and with this as a rope, come out of meditation while slowly, by increasing the amplitude of breath, to normal. Sustain the awareness with the rhythm of normal breathing, maybe between navel and throat.

2.5.11.6 Then change the awareness onto your fingers and toes and gently rub them. Slowly move your hands and rub your face and maybe your neck region.

2.5.11.7 Slowly bring the awareness of larger parts of your body and then try to move them. Come out in normal senses easily and patiently. Take your full time, no hurry.

2.5.11.8 Note: Be safe, slow, and silent. Do not jerk yourself, as it may cause harm.

2.5.11.9 In summary, do it slowly, tune into pranas and vibrational energy, then tune into slow breath. Then slowly fix your focus on the body with slow movements and then the larger body.

2.6 Helpful Progressive Signs

2.6.1 Sense of deep gratitude and happiness from within, which is acausal and unconditional in nature.

2.6.2 Various experiences of meditation occur, and ease of moving into objective and subjective awareness is attained.

2.6.3 Clear comprehension about un-conditionality. Ego-sense is dissolved as a center of activity.

2.6.4 Clear comprehension of faculties of life forms: mind, matter, consciousness, and vitality.

2.6.5 Feel prepared for the next step to advance mindfulness as a lifestyle.

3. Advance Practice into a Lifestyle —Mindful Living

3.1 Context

This is a very crucial step. Until this time, you cultivate the meditative qualities of concentration, various discriminative awareness, self- remembering, calmness, and wisdom; but everything is in a meditation room while sitting stable on a pillow. This is real, of course, but still an incubated experience.

Life experience is dynamic and multi-faceted. You live in a world out there with its social organizations built upon comparisons, competitions, and many non-sensible ideologies.

Like everybody else, a meditator also needs to act and live in the same world; therefore, mindfulness practice should become a lifestyle beyond the meditation room. For this, an engagement model is required to be tailored between meditative values and the world around them.

Hence this step focusses on: Cultivating mindfulness of dynamic activities and tailoring a social engagement model. This will require cultivating loving, kindness, and compassion values.

Meditation beyond the room requires mindfulness upon the relationship of—perception through active senses, mind-body objects during activity, subjective consciousness, and reactions as a unitary activity. Second, the essential thing is the mindfulness of the social environment. This is not for moralistic, ethical, or social compliance reasons, but to manage to live in such a way that outer society does not become a burden for your work.

Due to deep practice, you will have realized a psychosomatic transformation in you in terms of liberation from the grip of strong attachments or aversions; however, deep-seated impressions may surface at the time of activity. In this step, understanding patterns of activities, influences, underlying impressions, their roots, and reactions becomes important. Now, the meditator undertakes acute observation of actions involving perceptions and patterns of—thoughts, feelings, and sensations, which reflect the underlying impressions and the resulting reactions.

3.2 Goals

3.2.1 Cultivate mindfulness during an activity—perception, sensing, thinking, feeling, sensations, and reacting. And, the ability to witness these as one unitary function.

3.2.2 Cultivate mindfulness of hidden patterns and habits existing in the body-mind framework and move to their roots.

3.2.3 Cultivate stronger equanimity, compassion, and kindness.

3.2.4 Tailor an engagement model between your meditative values and the world around them.

3.3 Postural Guidelines

3.3.1 Not any specific posture, but it is helpful, to begin with, simple postures (explained later).

3.4. Helpful Attitude, Alerts and Cues

3.4.1 Attitude

3.4.1.1 Witness one task and its involved underlying activities, at one time.

3.4.1.2 Easy and equanimous in dynamic activities.

3.4.1.3 Selflessness, serenity, simplicity, and spontaneity to be practiced.

3.4.1.4 Being friendly, compassionate, and kind toward yourself and others.

3.4.1.5 Sensitivity of the social environment. It is required to integrate your values into the practical world.

3.4.2 Alerts

3.4.2.1 Don't be frustrated if you lose mindfulness during activities; instead, be mindfully compassionate towards yourself. A prayerful heart is very helpful.

3.4.2.2 Remember, it's your decision to value existential reality; therefore, you chose the path of inquiry and meditation. The people may not care for it, and you may face unsafe and challenging environments. Be mindful of social engagements around you.

3.4.2.3 Understand, others may not know your personal meditative situation while you are working intensely in your *being*. Hence, people may take you for granted or make fun out of you.

Make the discipline of compassion toward others and their actions.

3.4.2.4 Do not impose yourself on anyone or let anyone impose any effect on you. Do not overcharge yourself with any drama or vice- versa. Take it easy.

3.4.2.5 Come back to your inner mindfulness in your meditative posture, often.

3.4.2.6 There might be a slight chance that the mind starts the comparison, and you tend to think higher of yourself. This will create self-image which may gain solidity and create ego-static patterns on the mind. Beware of this aspect and use the mental torch to reveal it, and flush it out.

3.4.3 Cues

3.4.3.1 Make friends with other mindfulness meditators. A company of good motivating friends helps a lot in making it a lifestyle.

3.4.3.2 Integrate with the social world to the extent that it does not become a problem in your work. And, accordingly adopt the situational social attitudes—ethical, and moralistic.

3.4.3.3 Engage mindfully not to get involved in gossip and social drama.

3.4.3.4 Contribute to your deep, insightful values, wherever possible, have the courage to present your views but do not start canceling the social arrangements mindlessly.

3.5 Procedure

While keeping the regular discipline of sitting meditation practices, identify a few simple activities which are habitual or mechanical for you. In the beginning, choose individual, mundane, and daily repetitive activities. For example, walking, eating, lying down, showering, brushing your teeth, wearing clothes, writing, simple exercises, or hatha yoga. Keep the mental torch on activity.

Complete the cycle of one task at a time, and witness your actions and reaction patterns.

3.5.1 Here are a few examples:

3.5.1.1 While bathing, feel the warm or cold water falling on the skin. Witness the movements of hands. Witness the fresh feeling arising in the body. Witness the distractions coming in

mind, and re-align it with the activity. Be easy and equanimous.

3.5.1.2 While eating, do not feed your body before hunger arises. Witness the sensation of hunger, the arising intention to fulfill it. Witness the food and its perception via senses. Witness, what feeling comes about the food, lying before you. Witness the taste buds and respond to the thought of it, upon recognition. Witness the intention of the hand moving for food, picking it up, and bringing it to your mouth. Witness the entire eating process. Witness the sensation of fulfillment and reaction of pleasure acquired by the body before taking the next bite. Be easy and equanimous.

3.5.1.3 While doing yoga postures, witness the intention of stretches. Witness the moving body parts and body weight. Witness the sensation of pain and reactions to relieving the pain while moving the body. When coming out of poses, witness the pain dying away. Be easy and equanimous.

3.5.1.4 Once mindfulness exercises of simple physical tasks are done for a good time, take up the tasks that involve simple interactions with others. Self-remember while communicating, and witness the arising thoughts, feelings, and sensations. Be easy and equanimous.

3.5.1.5 While working in the world, witness the habitual patterns of thoughts, feelings, and sensations arising along with the perceptions. Witness their roots and reactions. Be easy and equanimous.

3.5.1.6 Witness the habitual patterns of complex decision-making, assumptions, assessment of the situation, process the information, and how you react. Witness the thoughts and feelings associated with the recognition of others' images and what sensation comes— Pleasurable or un-pleasurable. Witness the habits of types of values and drivers—power, affiliation, reason, or emotion, etc. you used while making decisions. Witness the roots and reactions, and be easy and equanimous.

3.5.2 As you grow mindfulness to the dynamic life, it becomes important to take this quality as a lifestyle, and engage with society accordingly. There is no predefined formula because it is contextual for everyone per situation. This entire book provides a picture of a meditator's lifestyle in various forms. However, few common ground rules can be shared here, as following:

3.5.2.1 Build a practical living philosophy of working principles and operating value system for yourself. How? Remember the 7W framework explained in the very beginning, use that.

3.5.2.2 Not all your values will be the same as of the world around you, so find the points of reconciliation and engage through that.

3.5.2.3 The mindless world divides itself into classes of independent and dependent *beings*, based on power, but wise cherish interdependence based on the experience of non-duality. It is rarely understood at its core but very important to understand for meditators.

3.5.2.3 Socially engage by understanding the quality of interdependence and togetherness. If you think something is wrong in society, then first relate with it before rectifying it.

Else, it will be a rude judgment, and you may end up in futile conflicts. Remember the fire in a jungle, and in a house-lamp have the same quality with one difference that a house-lamp is disciplined in using fire, whereas, in the jungle, it merely knows to burn and cause injury. Meditators are highly disciplined and efficient lamps of light. Their intention is never to hurt anyone, but only to heal.

3.5.2.4 Cultivate generosity, loving-kindness, and compassionate qualities to tailor a social engagement model. How? Create opportunities to act kindly for no return, send intense positive vibrations full of compassion to everyone—from near to far. Grow compassion as a lifestyle.

3.6 Helpful Progressive Signs

3.6.1 Deeply seated habitual patterns during activities get surfaced and get weakened.

3.6.2 Equanimity and awareness help in weeding out the patterns, and impressions and leaves you with a light and calm mind, even without any meditative effort.

3.6.3 A deep sense of joy and contentment is retained in the body-mind framework. Eventually, it becomes the default state of *being*.

3.6.4 Realization of a meaningful emptiness brings deep serenity. It's a very important stage.

3.6.5 Mindfulness becomes an unconditional lifestyle—living alone, or in public, it makes no difference.

4. Moving Beyond Mindfulness— Keep Moving On and On

4.1 Context

The realization of objective and subjective consciousness during static and dynamic activities ripens the meditator to move beyond mindfulness. In true sense, it is an alignment with existential intelligence—spontaneity, singularity, and suchness; and there are no milestones to measure. It's only moving on and on.

Simply living as a *being* "aware," and living most ordinarily as existence itself, is the key. There is experience, but not a separate experiencer, or there is action but not an actor. Therefore, it is difficult to formalize it in words through any language.

4.2 Goals

There are no specific goals. Instead, it's the time to retire and dissolve the mental torch of—intention, sustained effort, and awareness. Let awareness remain free. Why?

Remember, until this torch remains, there will be the tension of binding awareness with intention and attention, because truly awareness is nonlocal, and intention and attention are localization factors. This opposing force is the cause of inherent tension at a very subtle level. Now is the time to defocus the awareness. And, let it shine as-it-is as a pure function.

Living mindfully of things and processes happening in existence, and surrender to existence is a goal-less goal.

4.3 Postural Guidelines

4.3.1 No postural guidelines. Remain relaxed, easy, and alert.

4.4 Helpful Attitude, Alerts and Cues

4.4.1 Attitude

4.4.1.1 Constant self-witnessing and live spontaneously.

4.4.1.2 Living is almost like a freely flowing poem.

4.4.1.3 Happiness, joy, and contentment is default nature.

4.4.1.4 Realization of non-ownership in activities.

4.4.2 Alerts

4.4.2.1 Watch for any physical or mental activity that does not form solid patterns on *being*.

4.5 Procedure

4.5.1 Remain connected with native existence and live beyond the mind, which scribes your personal life story. Living life as the existence and not its worldly story is the key.

4.6 Helpful Progressive Signs

4.6.1 Boredom cannot come anytime. Meditation is continuously keeping you to move on and on.

4.6.2 Feeling of inner connectedness, oneness, and contentment.

4.6.3 Spontaneity, existential alignment, and acausal joy.

Conclusion

Was there anything or anyone before beginning?
Would there be anything or anyone after the end?
If yes, then there is no beginning and no end.
If no, then there is an empty *unknown* to know.

Both answers conclude in continuity,
of *known* and *unknown*,
knowing concludes in what we don't know,
And, unknowing gives birth to what we desire to know.

There is no end to our knowing,
Thus, the wise people say,
Charaiveti Charaiveti,
Keep going. Keep going.

When you started, you must had a mindset, now at this time after you have read, absorbed, and practiced the message(s) given in this book, once, twice, or maybe many times, you have a different mindset. Hopefully, you would have felt a shift in perception and consciousness.

It does not matter which thought, topic or meditation practice worked, what matters is the perfume of acausal happiness you carry with you in your consciousness and spread out. But your work doesn't stop with this book or any learning from outside; instead it expands in many ways.

Leave the book aside, live your real self, in love with existence. There is no other better way to know that this will also go away. So, keep going on, and keep going on.

Glossary

Being

Inner aliveness and animating life force, which acts as a foundation to mind and matter framework of living organisms. It is the vital energy behind the personality.

Reference: Appears in many chapters

Becoming

The makeup of human beings due to experiences of life, which is always in flux. This becoming gives a story to our life on earth.

Reference: Appears in many chapters

Bodhi

Bodhi is a state of wisdom attained by knowing the existential phenomenon. One who attains it can be called as Buddha.

Reference: Bodhi and The Pilgrim's caves

Causal Body

In the yogic tradition, the construct of a human being is said to have three bodies, namely, Gross, Subtle, and Causal bodies. All three bodies use various types of memories for the functioning of *being*. Out of these, the causal body is the deepest sheath that holds the essential impressions of a *being*. It is said that the Purifications of these bodies is the attainment of bliss and is the purpose of Yoga.

Reference: Appears in many chapters

Charaiveti

A Sanskrit word meaning keep going.

Reference: Appears in conclusion

Discriminative awareness

Our daily life offers a perception which is a muffled experience of objective and subjective consciousness. Therefore, our knowledge pool becomes murky, like mud in a turbulent lake. However, with the right meditative effort when the mind settles, one can filter the pure awareness from the qualities of objective experience. This state of mind is called discriminative awareness.

Reference: Four Step Meditation Technique

Dvija

In ancient Sanskrit, it means twice-born. The first birth is physical, and the second birth is spiritual.

Reference: The Hypocrite's Village

Equanimity

The state of mind which witnesses the nature of experience without getting caught up in it and react mindlessly. It does not mean in-action but an ability to act without ownership, attachment, or aversion for the given experience.

Reference: Appears in many chapters

Gross Body

In the yogic tradition, the construct of a human being is said to have three bodies, namely, Gross, Subtle, and Causal bodies. All three bodies use various types of memories for the functioning of *being*. Out of these, the gross body is the outermost sheath, which is made up of elements namely Being, Becoming and Beyond as, air, water, fire, space, and earth. This body is directly influenced by the environmental conditions and intake, E.g., food, air or water intake.

Reference: Appears in many chapters

Prana

In the yogic tradition, the term prana means vital energy. Everything we intake—food, water, or air; has pranas. Breathing is a pranic exercise through which we intake vital energy from existence.

Reference: Breathe to know

Subtle Body

In the yogic tradition, the construct of a human being is said to have three bodies, namely, Gross, Subtle, and Causal bodies. All three bodies use various types of memories for the functioning of *being* Out of these, the subtle body is the betwixt gross and causal sheath and provides a framework of mental elements like intellect, ego, emotions, and feelings.

Reference: Appears in many chapters

Sadho! Sadho!

A Buddhist practice mostly used by Vipassana meditators to say, well done! Or awesome!

Reference: Silence occurs...

Sankhya

One of the six schools of Hindu Philosophy. It is said to be the oldest one.

Reference: Shunyasati, The mindful Tea maker

Sati

Sati is a word in the Hindi language for awareness.

Reference: Shunyasati, The mindful Tea maker

Shunya

Shunya is a word in the Hindi language for being absolutely empty. It also means zero in numerology.

Reference: The mindful tea maker

Śūnyatā

Śūnyatā is a word in the Hindi language to indicate the quality of being empty.

Reference: Emptiness

Upanishad

These are collections of Ancient philosophical texts containing the core philosophy of human life, mostly aligned to the Hindu way of thinking. There are hundreds of them, but 108 are well recognized, out of which 18 are primary.

Reference: Appears in many chapters

Yoga-Darshan

One of the six schools of Hindu Philosophy. It is closely related to Sankhya Philosophy

Reference: Shunyasati, The mindful Tea maker

Endorsements

"Reading this book brings you to your essential nature, consciousness itself, and releases your highest wish—to vacate the mind's control. Shunya's use of verse and prose is a perfect medium for this transformational journey. His poetry shifts precisely through a myriad spectrum of language to convey the concise poetic expression of the essential truth of our Being and inspires the process of becoming That which takes us beyond our human mental conditions. The culmination of this book brings the reader to the highest dimension that Shunya calls emptiness, which is also the meaning of his pen name. His writings bring you—the reader, directly to the mindful awareness of one's eternal presence, which you already are, have always been, and always will be. I highly recommend you read this book and keep it close by for daily reflection."

Sherrie Wade (Shree),
Meditation Teacher, Author, and Director of Transformation
Meditation Online Institute

"In our current societal predicament, entropy seems to have gained a disturbing upper hand consistent with W.B. Yeats's "The Second Coming." To these extreme challenges comes Shunya's O Beloved. As an exploration of the lattice structures girding society, religion, business, healthcare, and even nations and their respective prescribed, pre-ordained solutions to temper life's ferment, Shunya reveals through Eastern anecdotes, poetic reflection and meditative insight the feasibility of self-revelation, gnosis, and renewal. Sourcing Buddha, Jung, Heraclitus, Lao Tzu, and Einstein, one encounters metaphorical inflections and a sincere distillation of the method to seek solace within and achieve inner peace. This sagacious work, perennial in scope, acknowledges our common humanity throughout history."

Dr. JG Roberts,
MD Surgical Phronesis, Inc.

"This book is studded with gems of timeless wisdom and enriched by the author's own deep reflections. The weaving of artwork, poetry, and prose makes this a unique and enchanting book for the seekers on the path of self-inquiry."

Imam Jamal Rahman,
author of "Spiritual Gems of Islam."

"Shunya has created a masterwork with his manuscript: O Beloved: Being, Becoming, and Beyond. He has drawn on his experience and familiarity with Eastern and Western cultures by blending the wisdom and spirituality of the former with the disciplined framework and practicality of the latter. He conveys confidence that living mindfully, fully aware of the moment is possible for everyone who is truly ready, and committed to discovering their true self. His poetry has been most effective by forcing me to slow down, open my heart and mind to his messages, and viscerally begin to experience the reality, joy, and grace of every moment. With that attraction, Rajesh presents practical, helpful steps for transitioning slowly, methodically, and patiently toward mastery of the building block practices of Breathing Exercises, Meditation Techniques, and a Mindfulness Lifestyle. The "how-to" steps for mastering these practices have given me the roadmap I need to make this spiritual turning a priority in my daily life."

John Hale, CEO Call of Compassion NW

"In this remarkable and rare book on self-inquiry, Shunya has carefully blended the Ancient wisdom, Modern day thinking, Art and Practical techniques to compose a rare jewel for the inquisitive souls. This book carries a powerful potential to help in the life-transforming investigation into the fundamental nature of human experience. It uncovers the unknown yet ever-present nature of our existential being by cultivating penetrating insights and simultaneously removing the conditionality, which causes the ignorance about our true "Self." This book unveils the DNA of a meditator's mindset without the baggage of esoteric language and provides the techniques with the right level of depth and simplicity. This book is a vital gift for our times."

Dr. I S Rai,
President, Universal Brotherhood Mission, USA

"I have come across O Beloved, at a time when I had embarked on a journey to have clarity on my meaning in life and the purpose of my life. First, Shunya has taken a complex, deep, and broad subject of the existence of human being, and wonderfully portrayed its various dimensions on both existential and physical levels. Difficult concepts are made clear via simple, easy to relate real-life scenarios, that makes it a breeze to read the book. This book serves as a great tool to understand our existence, decipher our daily struggles, and help serve as a backdrop to explore more into the inner causes of our worries about how to live. I am more fulfilling, aware of life filled with consciousness. I would consider myself an absolute beginner in understanding the nature of human being and philosophy per se, but the content is laid out so meticulously. The content presented via introductions and poems makes it an easy read as well. Added with the bonus content around meditations, this is a good all-rounder introduction that helps the reader get into the practice of living a balanced life."

Aromal Rajagopal,
Group CEO Caramatec Group of Companies

About Shunya

From an early age, **Shunya** (author's pen name, meaning *empty*) was deeply curious about the nature of reality underlying our body and mind framework. And, since his school days, he started exploring various philosophies and teachers with intense curiosity. Over time, he practiced several forms of yogic-meditative techniques, which he loves to share with other curious souls along with his personal learnings in simple and direct ways.

His self-defined goal is to reset human consciousness at the basic existential level where the nature of *experience* and *experiencer* is directly realized, in a natural way. Consequently, we live deeply connected with existence while celebrating our human incarnation.

He ardently believes that fundamentally human learning is three dimensional—in terms of *Philosophy, Science,* and *Arts.* And, all other branches can be subsidiary to these three. Everyone should earnestly exert to learn individually and develop collectively on these three dimensions of learning. The *Philosophical* dimension essentially and practically enables an inward-looking attitude, by which one progressively gains insight by moving from the manifested world towards the unified and undifferentiated nature of reality. The second dimension—*Science,* empowers the understanding of the manifested universe, identity, characteristics, and their inter-relationships. Thirdly, *Art* is conscious co-creation of the world to beautify our livelihood, and includes everything from a drawing book of a pre-school kid to building a nation or a spaceship. The shades of these three elements can be easily seen in his writings.

He is not associated with any religion or organization, nor does he hold any title or position in any form to promote his work. The entire work is humbly dedicated to all human beings irrespective of their religious, economic, cultural, or national backgrounds.

In the year 2015, he decided to express his learnings in the form of writings crystallized in books, poetry, and essays. The book: ***O Beloved- Being, Becoming, and Beyond*** is the first book in its series to achieve the goal, as mentioned earlier.

Lastly, he lives a very ordinary and simple life with his family in Seattle, WA, and has a full-time day job in a reputed organization.

More details can be found at www.shunyapragya.com
Connect at: Shunya@shunyapragya.com